T0194979

THE FAKE GOOD NEWS

WILLIAM (BILL) FRETWELL

WESTBOW
PRESS®
A DIVISION OF THOMAS NELSON
& ZONDERVAN

WestBow Press books may be ordered through booksellers or by contacting:

WestBow Press
A Division of Thomas Nelson & Zondervan
1663 Liberty Drive
Bloomington, IN 47403
www.westbowpress.com
1 (866) 928-1240

ISBN: 978-1-9736-9054-2 (sc)
ISBN: 978-1-9736-9053-5 (e)

Print information available on the last page.

WestBow Press rev. date: 07/28/2020

William (Bill) Fretwell is an ordained non-denominational minister and graduate of Grace Bible College of North Carolina. He also holds a MA in Community Counseling, from the University of North Alabama and a BSEd in Social Science, from Athens State University in Alabama. He is a Licensed Professional Counselor and a former school teacher. He has served in both the Marines and the Army. He has preached and taught the Bible for years, but is now primarily writing. He has been married to his wife Ruby for over 35 years and they now live in Wetumpka, Alabama. You may contact him at:

Bill Fretwell Ministries
160 Bristol Ln.
Wetumpka, AL 36092

Also see: www.billfretwellministries.com

CONTENTS

A BRIEF INTRODUCTION TO THIS BOOK

Dear believer,

The gospel of Jesus Christ has been called "the good news;" and just as there are counterfeits of just about everything good, there are counterfeits to our "good news." I call these counterfeits of our faith, the "fake good news." In the corrupt and agenda driven "fake news" of today, found on so many network news programs, the only real news and truth that gets through their network filtering process is that which fits their agendas. Their selection and editing of news, leaves out anything that contradicts their end game and any opinions that conflict with their politically correct, opinion poll tested, group think orthodoxy. These are considered "hate speech." Likewise, there is a similar war on truth and full disclosure in many of our churches. The false gospel of prosperity preachers pollutes our airwaves on both radio and television just about as much as the fake news does.

This book has four main themes that all relate to each other because each one discusses one form or another of false teaching or how to avoid falling for it. The first theme is about the false prosperity teachers/preachers/liars who butcher the gospel message and effectively promote the love of money over the love of God. Over half the book is on this spiritual cancer in our churches that needs to be cut out and discarded. The second theme is on spiritual bullies in our churches and denominations and how to deal with them effectively by setting scriptural boundaries. It discusses some of the "leaven of the pharisees," that is, doctrines of men that are taught as if they were the commandments of God.

The third theme is about the half-truths, which are really about one quarter truths, taught in most churches about tithing. I go into detail on all the scripture about tithing and related subjects, that when put together, shed a lot of light on the Mosaic (that given by Moses) law tithing system. You will gain a much clearer picture of how the Old Testament tithing system worked and how it does and does not apply to us today. The last of these four themes compliments the first three and serves as a guideline for studying the Bible on any topic/ doctrine and understanding it better than you ever have. It likewise helps you to not fall for error because you will know the truth much better. It is the Appendix. To borrow from the idea of the last being the first, you may want to read the Appendix first because it could help you get more out of the rest of the book.

We need to count the cost if we truly want to follow Christ; if we want relationship with him more than we want religion. There were those in Jesus' time who believed in him but would not say so because they were afraid of being thrown out of the temple. That situation has its equivalent today in believers who warm pews in churches the Holy Spirit is not always welcome in, if at all. They will not take a stand for what is right or against what they think is wrong in their church because they don't want to be thrown out of their church/ denomination (their temple). In this book I address the "lukewarm" believer who wants a comfortable religious life and in so doing, may become like one Jesus said in the book of Revelation, that he was about to spew out of his mouth.

When you combine these four Biblical themes, when you understand the principles found in them, and when you apply those principles in your life through a better understanding of the Word and the courage to stand on it by faith, you the reader have the ability to walk closer with God than you probably have since you first saw the light and experienced your "first love;" that fresh knowledge of Jesus that cleansed you from all unrighteousness and set you on a straight path. You have the ability to make your faith great again. May God work in you richly for your good and his glory.

Sincerely,
William Fretwell

APPRECIATION AND THANKS

I would like to thank the man who influenced me the most in the understanding of Biblical principles, the late Pastor Bill Caffey, of Texas. When I could not afford to go to Bible college, Bill, who had taught at a Bible college, became my pastor and he was my Bible college for an important period in my life. I would also like to thank the man who walks the principles of the Bible better than anyone I know, Pastor Daniel Martin. Many people have influenced me in positive ways, but these men are at the top.

Scripture quotation note: Unless otherwise stated, all scripture quoted in this book is from the New International Version of the Bible.

CHAPTER 1

PROSPERITY PREACHERS
CREATE SPIRITUAL POVERTY

D ear fellow Christian, it seems that today, more than ever
in my lifetime, there is an attack on the very fabric, basic
principles, and core values of our faith. This attack greatly
distorts the relationship we have with God the Father and our Lord Jesus
Christ. While the world attacks the church as a whole, and believers
individually, with all kinds of obviously carnal ideas, the attack I speak
of is from within the church, from those claiming to be leaders. This
attack I speak of is much more cunning and deceitful than the more
direct attacks of the political left with their evil agendas that are overtly
anti-Christian and hateful. It comes in the form of supposed "gospel"
principles. It comes from people who dress like, look like, and try to talk
like ministers. It is the so called "prosperity gospel" so popular in many
of our churches today.

This perverted "prosperity" gospel I am speaking of reduces the
good news of our Lord to a get rich quick scheme in which God has
been lowered to a mere "name it and claim it" "sugar daddy" to help
believers consume riches "upon their own lusts." Of course, it is not
openly explained that way. Many preachers who pollute our television

1

sets and radios with their twisted teachings have no time to teach solid doctrine on other issues (that is, assuming they know any) because it might cut into their bottom line of contributions, so they ignore solid doctrine and pour out one twisted message after another. It is really only one message presented in different ways.

These messages come from a variety of directions, but they almost always result in them saying something like, "If you give money to me, God will give more money and things to you." They mask their misleading message in nice "religious" sounding terms, knowing their hearers have "itching ears" to hear (II Tim. 4:3-4) and they put in a dab of scripture here and there for a more spiritual and less carnal flavor.

> [3] *For the time will come when people will not put up with sound doctrine. Instead, to suit their own desires, they will gather around them a great number of teachers to say what their itching ears want to hear.* [4] *They will turn their ears away from the truth and turn aside to myths.*

But it seems they conveniently leave out verses that would put the scripture they use in proper context and would give a balanced view on our relationship with God. They play on the scriptural ignorance and spiritual immaturity of their hearers and trust in the general carnality and naiveté of their flocks. Part of the reason for this book is to bring out scripture that shines light on and exposes this false teaching for what it is.

There are many scripture passages that warn us of people who had already come and who would come later, teaching false doctrine. Satan even tried to use scripture to tempt Jesus to sin but, was unsuccessful because Jesus knew all scripture and countered Satan's misuse of the Bible with an appropriate balancing passage (Mt. 4:4, 10-12). It is plain in II Tim. 2:15 that it is up to the individual believer to, *"study to show thyself approved, rightly dividing the word of truth."* We have to study, not only for **content**, but to make sure of what the **context** is and what the **covenant** is. In the next chapter of that book, in II Tim. 3:16, we see that all scripture is "God breathed," so we must not ignore any scripture if we want to be balanced and "rightly divide" what we believe.

2

[16] All Scripture is God-breathed and is useful for teaching, rebuking, correcting and training in righteousness,

The appendix to this book is mainly about these and other principles of Bible interpretation, also called hermeneutics. These principles are necessary knowledge so that the reader of the Bible can rightly divide and interpret the true meaning of scripture.

Those three things, content, context, and covenant (which I call the three Cs) are key to understanding the Word. We also need to know all scripture to some point, so that we know it at least well enough to be able to look up what the rest of the Bible teaches on a particular subject, like the subject of giving and finances, or eternal security, or any other point of doctrine. Of course, concordances help, whether online or in book form, but there is no substitute for knowing scripture well yourself.

Just because the Bible says something in one place, that does not mean that is all it has to say on the topic. When you take everything the Bible has to say on a subject and then look at the content, the context, and the covenant of each thing said, and blend it all together, you then begin to get a balanced picture of what God's view is on that doctrine. It is the ignorance of the whole Bible that allows people to accept half-truths or quarter-truths about the Word. As one preacher told me, half-truths are whole lies. It is extremely easy for false shepherds (who themselves may be partly deceived) to pull the wool over the eyes of ignorant sheep.

Peter tells us how shepherds of God's flock should act, in the following passage:

1 Peter 5:2

[2] Be shepherds of God's flock that is under your care, watching over them— not because you must, but because you are willing, as God wants you to be; not pursuing dishonest gain, but eager to serve;

Scripture is full, however, of warnings to the wise about shepherds that have other motivations.

2 Corinthians 11:14-15

> ¹⁴ *And no wonder, for Satan himself masquerades as an angel of light.* ¹⁵ *It is not surprising, then, if his servants also masquerade as servants of righteousness. Their end will be what their actions deserve.*

Matthew 7:15-16a

> ¹⁵ *"Watch out for false prophets. They come to you in sheep's clothing, but inwardly they are ferocious wolves.* ¹⁶ *By their fruit you will recognize them.*

Ezekiel 34:2-6

> ² *"Son of man, prophesy against the shepherds of Israel; prophesy and say to them: 'This is what the Sovereign LORD says: Woe to you shepherds of Israel who only take care of yourselves! Should not shepherds take care of the flock?* ³ *You eat the curds, clothe yourselves with the wool and slaughter the choice animals, but you do not take care of the flock.* ⁴ *You have not strengthened the weak or healed the sick or bound up the injured. You have not brought back the strays or searched for the lost. You have ruled them harshly and brutally.* ⁵ *So they were scattered because there was no shepherd, and when they were scattered they became food for all the wild animals.* ⁶ *My sheep wandered over all the mountains and on every high hill. They were scattered over the whole earth, and no one searched or looked for them.*

Ezekiel 34:10

> ¹⁰ *This is what the Sovereign LORD says: I am against the shepherds and will hold them accountable for my flock. I will remove them from tending the flock so that*

*the shepherds can no longer feed themselves. I will rescue
my flock from their mouths, and it will no longer be food
for them.*

In II Cor. 2:17, Paul refers to *"many"* preachers of his own time saying:

*[17] Unlike so many, we do not peddle the word of God for
profit. On the contrary, in Christ we speak before God
with sincerity, as those sent from God.*

Christ's half-brother, Jude, writes about some Old Testament versions
of this:

Jude 11

*[11] Woe to them! They have taken the way of Cain; they
have rushed for profit into Balaam's error; they have been
destroyed in Korah's rebellion.*

Balaam's story is given in Numbers chapters 22-25 and 31. This prophet's
desire for money eventually caused much harm to the Israelites. Besides
in the passage in Jude above, he is spoken of in II Pet. 2:15-16 and in
Rev. 2:14, if you care to look that up. Korah's rebellion is discussed in
Numbers 16.

In the 1960's Warner Brothers put out some entertaining cartoons
featuring a very large and shaggy sheepdog named Sam and his work-day
nemesis, Ralph the Wolf, who looked remarkably like a larger version
of Wile E. Coyote of Roadrunner fame. You can look up pictures of
them on the internet. Though the wolf and dog were friends away from
work, once they punched the time clock, Ralph had endless schemes
to capture a lamb from Sam's flock, but Sam (sometimes seen holding
a shepherd's crook) was always one or two steps ahead of him and
Ralph would suffer some form of non-lethal calamity that would stop
his scheme dead in its tracks. At the end of Ralph's frustrating, hungry,
and painful day, they would again punch the time clock and wish each
other a good night. The sheep were always safe.

Those were just cartoons of course, but, what would it have been like for the sheep if Sam had really been a wolf in sheepdog clothing or a wolf in shepherd's clothing? We have wolves in shepherd's clothing today, "shepherding" God's flock in many churches. They teach a message that is supposed to result in prosperity for their flock, but in truth leads to financial prosperity for the shepherds and leads to spiritual poverty, immaturity, shallowness, and a lack of fruit for the kingdom, in their flock; and that is just the good part. It also can lead to depression, confusion over Christian principles, and people leaving the church and the things of God in general, for a number of reasons. In the book, Church for the Unchurched, by George G. Hunter III, Abington Press, Nashville, 1996, he lists the constant teaching on giving more and more money as the number one reason people leave the church. I believe that is as true today as it was in the 1990's or more so.

These false prophets teach a twisted, unbalanced version of Christianity that is actually the opposite in its emphasis compared to what a balanced version of the gospel teaches. This backwards gospel's emphasis on finances runs many away from the church and reduces God, as I have said before, to some kind of "sugar daddy" who is supposedly there mainly to make Christians rich. It reverses the roles of God and believers. Instead of us serving God, it puts God in the role of being our servant. Jesus came as a servant to God, that was in part to set us an example and a standard of the attitude we should have toward God once we begin to follow him.

This "fake faith" or "fake good news" gospel stunts the spiritual growth of Christians who stay in these churches, in part by giving them a Biblical diet of only cake and pie type verses without balancing that with the meat and potatoes and spinach verses they need for spiritual strength and understanding. Even the cake and pie type verses often mean very different things than these false teachers say they do. For an example of this see the chapter later in this book about the "hundred fold return" teaching. The weakness that comes from these false doctrines makes the church goers much more susceptible to worldly influences that would drag them away from the flock and get them involved in a worldly lifestyle, if indeed they ever left it, since they came to belief through one of these false "prosperity" churches. See how the Apostle Paul addresses such thought and teaching in his first letter to Timothy.

1 Timothy 6:3-6

> [3] *If anyone teaches otherwise and does not agree to the sound instruction of our Lord Jesus Christ and to godly teaching,* [4] *they are conceited and understand nothing. They have an unhealthy interest in controversies and quarrels about words that result in envy, strife, malicious talk, evil suspicions* [5] *and constant friction between people of corrupt mind, who have been robbed of the truth and <u>who think that godliness is a means to financial gain.</u>*
>
> [6]*<u>But godliness with contentment is great gain.</u>*

The true path to prosperity and success as a believer involves faith for service in the Kingdom of God because a believer has received from God, and has further developed, the heart and desire of a servant, not a presumptive attitude. It is a faith that says God is and that he is a rewarder of those who diligently seek him (Heb. 11:6):

> [6] *And without faith it is impossible to please God, because anyone who comes to him must believe that he exists and that he rewards those who earnestly seek him.*

If we believe this, then we should believe that he wants to reward us for following him. THE PROBLEM IS, SOME THINK GOD SHOULD FOLLOW US INSTEAD OF US FOLLOWING HIM. I have only made a beginning on this topic. I will build much more on this theme in the next five chapters.

CHAPTER 2

DR. HAGIN MISSED IT BECAUSE THE MIDAS TOUCH WAS A CURSE

I read the little booklet written by the late Reverend, Doctor Kenneth Hagin in 1979, called "You Can Have What You Say!", published by Kenneth Hagin Ministries, Broken Arrow, Oklahoma. He was one of the early pioneers in the modern version of the "faith" or "prosperity" gospel movement. In this little book he teaches you to say what you want and to believe God will do it. He never mentions praying to ask God what his desire in a matter was or is, or to ask God what he wanted him (Hagin) to do. He does not mention seeking God's will one time in this book. Yes, I read it. Pastor Hagin later complained that people had taken what he said and went too far with it. Well, it is easy to see how they would. He later wrote a book called The Midas Touch, copyrighted by Faith Library Publications, Broken Arrow, OK, 2000, which was supposed to show a balance on the prosperity message and to teach some who had gone too far, in his opinion, where the balance was. A major problem with that book is that Hagin himself still did not seem to understand where the balance was and is. While he may have reigned in some of the worst beliefs and thinking on the financial prosperity question, he uses as an example of the other "extreme" position on finances, some people who supposedly think you should be "destitute" to be spiritual. Forgive me, but I have been in Christianity for almost 60 years and I don't know any of that latter group of people. I don't remember ever meeting any of them. I have read of Catholic monks who took vows of poverty, but nobody I know of in Protestant circles has.

You can certainly do without many things and still be very spiritual and good, but I don't know anyone who wants to be poverty stricken or to do without the necessities of life. Rev. Hagin made an effort in the Midas book to contrast those who want extreme wealth with some, who he says want abject poverty, doing without needed food and clothing and so forth. Again, I do not know where he found these "poverty extremists" who supposedly think you should do without things you need in order to make yourself spiritual; even the monks' vows of poverty do not cause them to do without necessities.

Frankly, this is the same tactic used by political liberals when they attack people who disagree with their views. The liberals think up the most extreme position possible on the right, one that nobody or almost nobody alive holds to or suggests, and try to assign that to the conservative in order to make the conservative sound irrational and extreme, even though that is not what the conservative is saying or believing at all.

Perhaps Dr. Hagin accidentally skipped over the following passage which continues from the passage in I Timothy quoted in Chapter 1:

1 Timothy 6:8-10

> *[8] But if we have food and clothing, we will be content with that. [9] Those who want to get rich fall into temptation and a trap and into many foolish and harmful desires that plunge people into ruin and destruction. [10] For the love of money is a root of all kinds of evil. Some people, eager for money, have wandered from the faith and pierced themselves with many griefs.*

Paul continues in vs. 17-19:

> *[17] Command those who are rich in this present world not to be arrogant nor to put their hope in wealth, which is so uncertain, but to put their hope in God, who richly provides us with everything for our enjoyment. [18] Command them to do good, to be rich in good deeds, and to be generous and willing to share. [19] In this way they will lay up treasure for themselves as a firm foundation for the coming age, so that they may take hold of the life that is truly life.*

Maybe Dr. Hagin thought Jesus and the apostles, including Paul, were extreme because they were content to only have what God provided and what they needed to do God's will, so they could accomplish a lot in the Kingdom of God and store away treasure in heaven. As in the case of political liberals attacking politically conservative positions, in The Midas Touch, Hagin exaggerated the position of people who attacked him for his unbalanced teaching and tried to make them seem ridiculous. I know people who have been through very tough times and have prayed to have their needs met and have gotten them met, myself included, but we were not going through tough times to make ourselves more spiritual. One of the reasons we go through trials is so we can learn to depend on God for our needs, not to develop greed.

James 1: 2-4

> [2] *Consider it pure joy, my brothers and sisters, whenever you face trials of many kinds,* [3] *because you know that the testing of your faith produces perseverance.* [4] *Let perseverance finish its work so that you may be mature and complete, not lacking anything.*

I know Dr. Hagin is dead now, but someone should have reminded him when he was writing The Midas Touch, that the golden touch of King Midas was a curse, not a blessing to him in the end. If they had, he might have considered another title for his book.

These truths are partly why I call the so-called "prosperity gospel," the spiritual poverty gospel. That is, you can't take worldly wealth with you, but you can lay up for yourselves treasures in heaven by doing what God leads you to do for the Kingdom of God. There are, however, right now or "now-time" benefits to serving God. These include having peace in your hearts and feeling close to God, which all the money in the world can't buy. I was a teenager in the 1960's and there was a song back then by the rock and roll group, Paul Revere and the Raiders, called "Kicks," which was about someone wasting their life looking for kicks with drugs, sex, etc. In the chorus, he sang "and all the kicks "aint" bringin' you peace of mind ..." He was surely right. True happiness and peace of mind can't be found in all the riches one can possess. It can only be found through being involved with doing what God puts in one's heart to do once we have sought him with all our hearts and minds for what that is. Truly, we must *"seek first the Kingdom of God and all His righteousness"* and all we need will be added to us (Mt. 6:33 paraphrase).

A VOICE OF AGREEMENT FROM "RELIGIOUS" PSYCHOLOGY

As a counselor I know that if a person gets all the worldly things they think they want, but doesn't have that proper relationship of service to and friendship with God, they will find there is a void in their life that seems even emptier than before they got all the things they sought.

Some psychologists would call this an existential vacuum. Dr. Viktor Frankl, was the famous Jewish psychiatrist who came up with the idea of the "will to meaning," as opposed to the "will to pleasure" (Freud), and the "will to power" (Adler). Frankl's ideas were often criticized by secular people in psychology as being the same as religion. In his book, Man's Search for Meaning, Beacon Press, Boston Mass., 1959, 1962, 1984, and in other writings, Frankl taught something that agrees with the Bible; that is, that we have to be aligned with doing what we think is pure, right, and of good moral value in order to be content. In my opinion, following God's plan for you as he reveals it, is the best way possible to do this. Dr. Frankl had to test his theories in Nazi concentration camps during WWII, where he was imprisoned and where his wife and both parents perished. Reading Man's Search for Meaning is a very rewarding, uplifting and motivating task for anyone who has yet to read it.

GOD HAS A PLAN FOR US

In Jer. 29:11 Jeremiah writes about God having a positive plan for the Jews, but in the verses just before that, he warns them not to listen to the false prophets that he (God) has not sent, nor to their dreams, which they (the Jews) encouraged the prophets to have. Too many people in too many churches are seeking these pitiful half-baked preachers of prosperity because they prophecy or teach "smooth" words. See Isaiah 30: 9-13 about lying prophets and their willing listeners.

> For these are rebellious people, deceitful children,
> children unwilling to listen to the LORD's instruction.
> [10] They say to the seers,
> "See no more visions!"
> and to the prophets,
> "Give us no more visions of what is right!
> Tell us pleasant things,
> prophesy illusions.
> [11] Leave this way,
> get off this path,

and stop confronting us
with the Holy One of Israel!"
[12] *Therefore this is what the Holy One of Israel says:*
"Because you have rejected this message,
relied on oppression
and depended on deceit,
[13] *this sin will become for you*
like a high wall, cracked and bulging,
that collapses suddenly, in an instant.

In these types of churches, I think, the blame for error goes about 35% to the flock and 65% to the ministers. The smaller percentage is for the foolish flock that tolerates or even encourages the false teaching and the rest is for the "Balaamite" type shepherds. I don't want to get side-tracked now on who is responsible for error taking hold in a body of believers because I am talking about God having a plan for us and how not to miss it, but the false shepherds/prophets/teachers are only partly to blame.

God does have a plan for us if we seek him, a plan of service for us (each individual). I will quote the passage from Jeremiah that both "prosperity" preachers and I use:

Jeremiah 29:11

> [11] *For I know the plans I have for you," declares the* LORD,
> *"plans to prosper you and not to harm you, plans to give*
> *you hope and a future.*

This is a wonderful passage, but to see the full truth of it, we have to balance it with other passages on the same topic from scripture, like the following one Jesus said:

Matthew 16:24-27

> [24] *Then Jesus said to his disciples, "Whoever wants to*
> *be my disciple must deny themselves and take up their*
> *cross and follow me.* [25] *For whoever wants to save their*

life will lose it, but whoever loses their life for me will find it. ²⁶ What good will it be for someone to gain the whole world, yet forfeit their soul? Or what can anyone give in exchange for their soul? ²⁷ For the Son of Man is going to come in his Father's glory with his angels, and then he will reward each person according to what they have done.

WHAT IS SUCCESS FOR A CHRISTIAN?

If God has a plan, a mission for us, then we are only successful in our Christian life when we line up with him and his will for our life. To miss his plan is to miss full success. We are successful when we seek to carry out his mission for us and apply ourselves to that work. That is what success is as a Christian; it is being in the center of his will, in the center of his mission for us as individuals, at all times. This is where we find that part of his riches that come to us in this life, the joy, peace, patience and the other fruits of the Spirit. We lose these when we get out of his plan for us and all the worldly goods and riches can't get them back for us. Only the return to his will and plan, can do that.

CHAPTER 3

WHERE GOD GUIDES, GOD PROVIDES
(BUT NOT ALWAYS THE WAY WE WANT)

1 John 5:14-15

> *14 This is the confidence we have in approaching God:*
> *that if we ask anything <u>according to his will</u>, he hears us.*
> *15 And if we know that he hears us— whatever we ask—we*
> *know that we have what we asked of him.*

This is another Bible passage sometimes used by prosperity teachers, but they sort of side step the "his will" part or they say something like "Jeremiah 29 says it is his will for you to prosper, so go ahead and pray for that new house or Cadillac; oh, and by the way, if you send us a seed faith pledge today, I believe that will guarantee God will answer that request." How many times have you heard something like that on television or on the radio?

When you balance this passage in I John 5 with the following passage from James, you see the I John verses really teach us that if we know it is his will to get something because we have to have it to do what we know he has put in our hearts and minds and spirits to do, then we can have confidence in praying for it. For instance, I have prayed for a job at times when I did not have one because I knew it was God's will for me to work. I also prayed for the job God wanted me to have. Most of the time, however, people are not praying for God's will, that is, to be provided with what they need to do his will. Instead they pray for their own will to get something they want so they can have pleasure in or with it. James 4:3-4 tells us that we will not get that thing, and tells us why not. It would not even be good for us.

James 4: 3-4

> ³ When you ask, you do not receive, because you ask with wrong motives, that you may spend what you get on your pleasures.

> ⁴ You adulterous people, don't you know that friendship with the world means enmity against God? Therefore, anyone who chooses to be a friend of the world becomes an enemy of God.

Do you see how James 4 brings clarity and balance to this doctrine of what to pray for and why? Compare that passage with the following about Moses.

Hebrews 11:24-26

> ²⁴ By faith Moses, when he had grown up, refused to be known as the son of Pharaoh's daughter. ²⁵ He chose to be mistreated along with the people of God rather than to enjoy the fleeting pleasures of sin. ²⁶ He regarded disgrace for the sake of Christ as of greater value than the treasures of Egypt, because he was looking ahead to his reward.

If you have or have had children and they asked for something you knew they should not have, hopefully you did not give it to them. You withheld it because you were older and wiser and knew it would be a problem for them. The way Kenneth Hagin wrote in "You Can Have What You Say!", the kids get to tell the parent what they are going to get. GOD DOES NOT RAISE SPIRITUAL BRATS! If capital letters are the equivalent of yelling then good! That is what I was going for. The parents know better what is good or bad for their kids than the kids do. In the case of God the Father, he knows exactly what he wants us to have, how much of it, when it should come, and all the other details. If we have half a spiritual brain, if we have any wisdom, we will seek him to find out his plan for us and will then pray hard (with our whole heart) for what we need to get that job done.

To break it down, if God tells you to do something that involves transportation and you don't have any, don't get stupid and start telling God what kind of Cadillac you want. Ask him if he wants you to walk or what other way should you use to get there. If you believe he is telling you to go by car, then ask him to provide the vehicle. The answer might come back that he wants you to get a job and save up and buy the one that, after more prayer, he shows you. He might say to just rent one for the trip. He might put into someone's heart to give you an old car, maybe one that needs some fixing, but maybe not. Where God guides, he will also provide, but not necessarily the way we think or would like him to, but it will be what is for our best in the long run (his plan for us). I will tell you I have had two used cars given to me by other Christians when I was young and even though both cars needed work, they were blessings. Isaiah 55:8-9 tells us that God's thoughts are way above our thoughts. It is foolish for us to think otherwise. Jesus did a lot of walking and we know at least once, he rode on a donkey. He will ride on a white horse one day, but that was not in God the Father's plan 2000 years ago and Jesus set us an example of following God's will.

Once a believer realizes that what is in their own (even selfish) best interest is to be in God's plan, and believes it with all their soul and with all their being, and that when he/she seeks first God's righteousness, God adds the things we need to that (Mt. 6:33) then he/she won't be asking for what their worldly mind wants, but for what their spiritual being and their transformed mind needs.

Other very important passages stated by Jesus himself, that these false teachers seem to not be aware of and that teach us about trusting in God's plan for us follow.

Matthew 6:19-21

> [19] "Do not store up for yourselves treasures on earth, where moths and vermin destroy, and where thieves break in and steal. [20] But store up for yourselves treasures in heaven, where moths and vermin do not destroy, and where thieves do not break in and steal. [21] For where your treasure is, there your heart will be also.

Matthew 6:28-33

> [28] "And why do you worry about clothes? See how the flowers of the field grow. They do not labor or spin. [29] Yet I tell you that not even Solomon in all his splendor was dressed like one of these. [30] If that is how God clothes the grass of the field, which is here today and tomorrow is thrown into the fire, will he not much more clothe you—you of little faith? [31] So do not worry, saying, 'What shall we eat?' or 'What shall we drink?' or 'What shall we wear?' [32] For the pagans run after all these things, and your heavenly Father knows that you need them.[33] But seek first his kingdom and his righteousness, and all these things will be given to you as well.

I next want to quote out of sequence, a verse that came earlier in Matthew chapter six, because I want to elaborate on it a little.

Matthew 6:11

> [11] Give us today our daily bread.

Instead of praying for our daily bread so we can do God's will in our lives, prosperity preachers promote a self-centered, rather than God and others centered life. They promote a self-seeking rather than a God seeking theology that results in the kind of spiritual poverty (regardless of worldly wealth) that is spoken of by Jesus regarding the lukewarm but worldly wealthy church at Laodicea in the book of Revelation.

Revelation 3:14-19

> [14] "*To the angel of the church in Laodicea write:*
>
> *These are the words of the Amen, the faithful and true witness, the ruler of God's creation.* [15] *I know your deeds, that you are neither cold nor hot. I wish you were either one or the other!* [16] *So, because you are lukewarm— neither hot nor cold—I am about to spit you out of my mouth.* [17] *You say, 'I am rich; I have acquired wealth and do not need a thing.' But you do not realize that you are wretched, pitiful, poor, blind and naked.* [18] *I counsel you to buy from me gold refined in the fire, so you can become rich; and white clothes to wear, so you can cover your shameful nakedness; and salve to put on your eyes, so you can see.*
>
> [19] *Those whom I love I rebuke and discipline. So be earnest and repent.*

You see that the rich people were called in verse 17, "*wretched, pitiful, poor, blind and naked*" by Jesus. That is what I mean by saying that those who seek wealth and possessions instead of heavenly prosperity are in spiritual poverty. They are not seeking God. They are seeking things. That is why they are lukewarm, neither hot nor cold and why Jesus says what he does about them. According to one Bible commentary I have read, Laodicea was famous for its cloth industry, especially wool, and for a medical school and the production of an eye salve. Jesus evidently alluded to these things, first by recommending they buy white clothes (the righteousness of the saints, see Rev. 19:8 below) and a type of eye salve that instead of helping their earthly eyes, would instead, let them see spiritual truths.

Revelation 19:8

> [8] *Fine linen, bright and clean, was given her to wear.*"
> *(Fine linen stands for the righteous acts of God's holy people.)*

You may wonder how they were going to buy something from Jesus without money. Money is not the currency God deals with and there is no exchange rate from dollars into spiritual currency. The eternal blessings we save up for ourselves come from righteous acts; that is serving God, not our own carnal natures.

Again, you may wonder about the feasibility of being able to know God's plan for your life. Scripture teaches us that God shares his plans with his friends and that we can be his friends. We can be FRIENDS WITH GOD, knowing his ways/paths, at least to the point that we need to know. See the following passages:

Exodus 33:11

> [11] The LORD would speak to Moses face to face, as one speaks to a friend. Then Moses would return to the camp, but his young aide Joshua son of Nun did not leave the tent.

Psalm 103:7

> [7] He made known his ways to Moses,
> his deeds to the people of Israel:

2 Chronicles 20:7

> [7] Our God, did you not drive out the inhabitants of this land before your people Israel and give it forever to the descendants of Abraham your friend?

James 2:23

> [23] And the scripture was fulfilled that says, "Abraham believed God, and it was credited to him as righteousness," and he was called God's friend.

John 15:14-15

> [14] *You are my friends if you do what I command.* [15] *I no longer call you servants, because a servant does not know his master's business. Instead, I have called you friends, for everything that I learned from my Father I have made known to you.*

So not only did God treat Abraham and Moses as his friends, but Jesus considers us believers today his friends if we try to do what he commands. He also says he will let us know his will, his business.

FALSE GUIDANCE

Because I believe in the baptism in the Holy Spirit and the Pentecostal gifts still being available for us today, there is something especially embarrassing for me to deal with regarding the prosperity preachers. That is most, if not all of the prosperity teachers claim to have received this experience. If they have received this baptism they should be very sensitive to the guidance of the Holy Spirit, his direction and leading in their lives. Yet, they seem to me to be less in tune with him than anyone but the straight cults. Instead of promoting God's will, they are promoting their pocketbooks. Instead of being led by God, as I have said, they want to lead him. They are not then the friends of God according to the description just given in John 15 and their "gospel" is a false gospel, a gospel of spiritual poverty. To accept this poverty gospel, the gospel of worldly goods instead of treasures in heaven, is extremely foolish. To accept friendship with the world instead of friendship with Jesus by drawing close to him and receiving his guidance and direction through the Holy Spirit, is very short-sighted. To accept the temporary worldly satisfaction of what we can figuratively call Esau's bowl of lentil stew (Gen. 25:34) instead of the birthright that is ours, the birthright of being close to God and to walk in his ways and his will, is truly foolish. These things are more pleasing to the enemies of the cross than its friends. Think about how worldly people love to point to the financial wealth of certain preachers as evidence of hypocrisy in the Christian faith. Unfortunately, they are mainly right about that.

MORE ON FRIENDSHIP WITH GOD

Moses met with God face-to-face daily in prayer. His face shown from the glory and he had to cover his face (Ex 34:35). The Apostle Paul wrote about how we can be like Moses in our relationship with God (2 Cor. 3:7-18). Verse 18 emphasizes this.

II Corinthians 3:18

> [18] *And we all, who with unveiled faces contemplate the Lord's glory, are being transformed into his image with ever-increasing glory, which comes from the Lord, who is the Spirit.*

You see, friendship begets fellowship. Recount the benefits of humble righteousness and communion with God, of dying to self, of becoming what he wants one to be – which is worth more in the light of history and eternity than anyone can have or be, in any other way. The comparison of the lentil stew versus the birthright, of Jacob and Esau is an appropriate one for this topic, as is the fact that Esau later repented in tears that he had given up the opportunity he'd been given of far more than that bowl of lentils. Read the story from Genesis:

Genesis 25:30-34

> [30] *He said to Jacob, "Quick, let me have some of that red stew! I'm famished!" (That is why he was also called Edom.)*
> [31] *Jacob replied, "First sell me your birthright."*
> [32] *"Look, I am about to die," Esau said. "What good is the birthright to me?"*
> [33] *But Jacob said, "Swear to me first." So, he swore an oath to him, selling his birthright to Jacob.*

³⁴ Then Jacob gave Esau some bread and some lentil stew.
He ate and drank, and then got up and left.
So, Esau despised his birthright.

The author of Hebrews also talks about this:

Hebrews 12:16-17:

> *¹⁶ See that no one is sexually immoral, or is godless like*
> *Esau, who for a single meal sold his inheritance rights as*
> *the oldest son. ¹⁷ Afterward, as you know, when he wanted*
> *to inherit this blessing, he was rejected. Even though he*
> *sought the blessing with tears, he could not change what*
> *he had done.*

Just like Esau, prosperity teachers/preachers want and teach physical gratification. In the temporary, short-term situation, to Esau the bowl of stew was more important to him than his birthright (the double portion of the inheritance from all that Isaac his father had, which went along with his being the oldest son). Esau had been out in the fields and came in very hungry but, was not starving or anywhere near death.

We have such a choice as believers today. We have a choice of walking in worldly foolishness, in spiritual shallowness, and distance from the richness of the Spirit of God or of walking with Jesus as our Lord and friend. Seeking his will regularly, spending time in prayer as Moses did daily, is a sure way to start on the right road. Then, after learning his will for us, doing his will is the same as picking up our cross so we do not lose our eternal rewards.

We have talked already about what Jesus said in Mt. 6 about putting your treasure in heaven (vs. 19) and not being able to serve two masters, God and money (vs. 24). We also looked at James 4:4 where James writes that friendship with the world is enmity with God. We can be truly rich and be a friend of Jesus, or we can seek economic wealth here and be a friend of the world. You can't do both. You must decide. Jesus also said that the greatest among you will be your servant (Mt. 23:11-12). It is this humbling and taking on the heart of a servant that is vital to becoming great in the kingdom of God. We are called to be servants, not to be served, to be warriors in spiritual warfare for the kingdom of God, not armchair generals sitting back and watching the fight someone else fights for us. There are many examples in the Old Testament of God fighting for his people, but in each case, the people of God had to at least suit up and show up the way God told them to.

The story of the rich young ruler (Lk. 18:18-23 and Mt. 19:16-30) describes a seemingly nice young man who lost out on becoming great in God's kingdom because it involved obeying Jesus and in selling all he had and giving it to the poor and following Christ. He had great wealth and decided he liked that more. St. Francis of Assisi was a wealthy young man who gave up his worldly wealth to serve God by helping the poor. He felt revulsion when he went to Rome to ask the Pope for permission to start a religious order. Everywhere he looked he saw extravagance and riches. He stopped making his request to the Pope and started preaching against the riches and used the beatitudes of Jesus from Matthew to do so. He was a rich young ruler, so to speak, who chose rightly. Though I am not Catholic, I believe his life of service to Christ, like that of Mother Teresa's, won them both riches in heaven.

It is plain to me that what prosperity preachers teach is really poverty teaching, and that giving up the love of money for Christ, is true prosperity. The things we need to have, to do the will of God are already promised to us if we seek first his kingdom and his righteousness, he says these will be added to us. We also saw that there is nothing wrong with asking for things we know are in his will and if that is all we ask, we can have confidence he hears us and that he will respond. We find that greed is a sin and seeking after what is not true wealth is foolish. When Solomon prayed for wisdom and the like, to help him become a good ruler of the great people Israel, God said because you asked for these things and not for wealth, I will provide you with both.

1 Kings 3:1-15:

> 3 *Solomon made an alliance with Pharaoh king of Egypt and married his daughter. He brought her to the City of David until he finished building his palace and the*

temple of the LORD, and the wall around Jerusalem. ² The people, however, were still sacrificing at the high places, because a temple had not yet been built for the Name of the LORD. ³ Solomon showed his love for the LORD by walking according to the instructions given him by his father David, except that he offered sacrifices and burned incense on the high places.

⁴ The king went to Gibeon to offer sacrifices, for that was the most important high place, and Solomon offered a thousand burnt offerings on that altar. ⁵ At Gibeon the LORD appeared to Solomon during the night in a dream, and God said, "Ask for whatever you want me to give you."

⁶ Solomon answered, "You have shown great kindness to your servant, my father David, because he was faithful to you and righteous and upright in heart. You have continued this great kindness to him and have given him a son to sit on his throne this very day.

⁷ "Now, LORD my God, you have made your servant king in place of my father David. But I am only a little child and do not know how to carry out my duties.⁸ Your servant is here among the people you have chosen, a great people, too numerous to count or number. ⁹ So give your servant a discerning heart to govern your people and to distinguish between right and wrong. For who is able to govern this great people of yours?"

¹⁰ The Lord was pleased that Solomon had asked for this. ¹¹ So God said to him, "Since you have asked for this and not for long life or wealth for yourself, nor have asked for the death of your enemies but for discernment in administering justice, ¹² I will do what you have asked. I will give you a wise and discerning heart, so that there will never have been anyone like you, nor will there ever be.[13] Moreover, I will give you what you have not asked for—both wealth and honor—so that in your lifetime you will have no equal among kings. [14] And if you walk in obedience to me and keep my decrees and commands as David your father did, I will give you a long life." [15] Then Solomon awoke—and he realized it had been a dream.

I have written already about what Jesus said to the Laodicean church in Revelations 3. I want to requote that and then compare it to what he says to the church at Smyrna.

Rev. 3:14-19:

[14] "To the angel of the church in Laodicea write:

These are the words of the Amen, the faithful and true witness, the ruler of God's creation. [15] I know your deeds, that you are neither cold nor hot. I wish you were either one or the other! [16] So, because you are lukewarm— neither hot nor cold—I am about to spit you out of my mouth. [17] You say, 'I am rich; I have acquired wealth and do not need a thing.' But you do not realize that you are wretched, pitiful, poor, blind and naked. [18] I counsel you to buy from me gold refined in the fire, so you can become rich; and white clothes to wear, so you can cover your shameful nakedness; and salve to put on your eyes, so you can see.

[19] Those whom I love I rebuke and discipline. So be earnest and repent.

Jesus likewise refers to the church at Smyrna as being rich even though they were poor regarding worldly wealth:

Rev. 2: 8-11:

> [8] *"To the angel of the church in Smyrna write:*
> *These are the words of him who is the First and the Last,*
> *who died and came to life again.* [9] *I know your afflictions*
> *and your poverty—yet you are rich! I know about the*
> *slander of those who say they are Jews and are not, but*
> *are a synagogue of Satan.* [10] *Do not be afraid of what you*
> *are about to suffer. I tell you, the devil will put some of*
> *you in prison to test you, and you will suffer persecution*
> *for ten days. Be faithful, even to the point of death, and*
> *I will give you life as your victor's crown.*
>
> [11] *Whoever has ears, let them hear what the Spirit says to*
> *the churches. The one who is victorious will not be hurt*
> *at all by the second death.*

To bring up some pop culture and recent television programs and apply those to this situation, it seems we have some "zombie" churches today. These are churches that have a reputation for being alive, but are really dead or dying. The vultures or wolves in shepherds' clothing are picking the bones of the flock even while their twisted emphasis messages are making the flock weak and sickly and even running them off from what should be the safety of a flock.

According to the prosperity teacher/preacher's viewpoint, the Smyrna Christians just did not have enough faith and/or were not giving enough to God or else they would have been rich financially. Which of the apostles of Christ were wealthy? None were! That is right! If godliness is a means to financial gain, though scripture says it is not, then at least some of them would have been rich, correct? Well, they were and are rich, but not by this world's estimation. They were rich in good deeds, in faith, in sufferings for Christ and other things. These hardships and sufferings for doing the will of God were what earned them treasures in heaven. They were also rich in this life in things like peace of mind, a clear conscience, and in their relationship with Christ. I have known a number of financially wealthy people during my life and, as I have alluded to before, I have never known a very content one. St. Paul listed gladly his bank account contents when he shared about his beatings, his being shipwrecked, his being stoned, his hunger, lack of clothing, having suffered cold, and his having to deal with false brethren and hostile Jews.

2 Corinthians 11:23-33:

> [23] *Are they servants of Christ? (I am out of my mind to talk like this.) I am more. I have worked much harder, been in prison more frequently, been flogged more severely, and been exposed to death again and again.* [24] *Five times I received from the Jews the forty lashes minus one.* [25] *Three times I was beaten with rods, once I was pelted with stones, three times I was shipwrecked, I spent a night and a day in the open sea,* [26] *I have been constantly on the move. I have been in danger from rivers, in danger from bandits, in danger from my fellow Jews, in danger from Gentiles; in danger in the city, in danger in the country, in danger at sea; and in danger from false believers.* [27] *I have labored and toiled and have often gone without sleep; I have known hunger and thirst and have often gone without food; I have been cold and naked.* [28] *Besides everything else, I face daily the pressure of my concern for all the churches.* [29] *Who is weak, and I do not feel weak? Who is led into sin, and I do not inwardly burn?*

It is not the easy times that win us honor and treasure with God, it is being a good soldier in the face of difficulties; following God's orders when it is a sacrifice to do so. Do you really believe Kenneth Hagin, Kenneth Copeland, Creflo Dollar, or any other prosperity preacher will have anything like the Apostle Paul's reward in heaven? I am not even sure some of these people will get in. If they do, I think they will be like a *"smoldering branch plucked from the flames"* (Zech. 3:2).

When the then newly elected President, John F. Kennedy, told Americans in 1961 to "Ask not what your country can do for you, ask what you can do for your country," he was talking to a largely pre-welfare society. Most Americans then believed they owed this country some type of loyalty and service. Likewise, in my youth, I think most people thought, rightly so, of a Christian life as being one devoted to God and to his service. Today's citizen, as opposed to the Americans of my youth (our much more shallow and self-centered society of today), feels entitled to more and more and feels obligated to do less and less. That is how these "prosperity" church Christians seem to be to me. They are largely speaking, a whiney, immature, and really rather pitiful example of spiritual warriors. As Paul once wrote to the Corinthian believers, *"I could not address you as mature, but as worldly"* (I Cor. 3:1). These "faith" church believers seem in that category too. As I have mentioned already, though I put most of the blame for the success and popularity of the prosperity message on the shoulders of the wolf-like shepherds, there is blame to go around for the sheep, especially to those that have been in the faith longer. By failing to study the Bible for themselves and by failing to question teachings that do not lineup with a balanced view of the Word, they have to share some responsibility for their own deception.

At a time when our world may be facing another world war in the near future, I have trouble thinking about this crop of Americans, this "me generation," standing up to that as well as the "greatest generation" did. Likewise, when trouble and hardship come the way of believers today, will these shallow and weak "prosperity" Christians have deep enough roots and mature enough minds to stand up under the pressure? Or, when trouble and/or hardship comes, will they fall away, to their own destruction?

We intuitively understand that for a military person to be tough and ready for combat, they have to train extremely hard. It is not fun to do this, I know. I spent a couple of difficult years in the Marines during the Vietnam Conflict and every trainer we had in our infantry school had been to Vietnam at least once. They pushed us hard because they knew what it was like over there and they wanted us to survive the experience if we went. It would have been cruel of those NCO's to halfway train us and just ship us into combat. It would have been easier on them to ease up and they would surely have been more popular with us trainees if they had, but in the end, I appreciated what they did because I knew the reason it was done. I never had to go to combat, but if I had, I was about as ready as one could get without actual combat experience. We understand also that to win the higher level of medals, a military person has to do something difficult, brave, and so forth. It is the difficult things we do for God that earn treasures in heaven, not the easy things. These are some true riches, not sitting on a fat bank account down here or driving a fancy car, living in a mansion and dressing to the 9s.

The truth is that being a good soldier or Marine or other service member, and being in a combat unit that has been proven capable of undergoing difficult assignments and accomplishing the mission, will get you more assignments that are tough. This is not as punishment, but is an opportunity given based on proven past success.

In Mt. 25: 28-30, in the parable of the talents (coins) there is an example in the end when the one piece of money was taken away from the lazy servant and given to the one who had ten because he had used them profitably. By applying this parable to believers, God is showing us an example that, as Christ was a servant, so we are servants of God; and as Jesus earned glory by obeying the tough requests of God the Father, so we earn heavenly riches by serving God, not by being served. New believers often have many needs that God meets because they are like *"newborn babies"* (I Peter 2:2) and God treats them as such. He still does not meet their greed, just their needs. For those who are older in the faith, however, he expects them to become solders, workers, laborers in the harvest field. He still meets their needs but, expects those needs to be in line with fulfilling his will. It is the service we perform for God that earns us treasures in heaven and promotes us within God's economy. The prosperity message reverses this and tells us, in so many words, that God is our servant to make us rich in worldly finances. This is why, I believe one of the poorest people in worldly wealth mentioned in the Bible, the Apostle Paul, is one of the richest in heavenly treasures today.

SPIRITUAL RICHES

So, what are spiritual riches? One form of being spiritually rich is that of being rich in good deeds as mentioned in I Timothy:

1 Timothy 6:18-19:

> [18] *Command them to do good, to be rich in good deeds, and to be generous and willing to share.* [19] *In this way they will lay up treasure for themselves as a firm foundation for the coming age, so that they may take hold of the life that is truly life.*

In James 2:1-9 quoted next, we see the teaching that it is wrong to discriminate against poor people and in vs. 5 it says God has chosen the poor to be rich in faith. The prosperity or "faith" teachers, as they are wrongly called, say the opposite in their twisted theology. They say that if you are poor, you don't have enough faith. While it is not a sin by itself to be rich, it is certainly not one to be poor. Please read for yourself:

James 2: 1-9:

> 2 *My brothers and sisters, believers in our glorious Lord Jesus Christ must not show favoritism.* [2] *Suppose a man comes into your meeting wearing a gold ring and fine clothes, and a poor man in filthy old clothes also comes in.* [3] *If you show special attention to the man wearing fine clothes and say, "Here's a good seat for you," but say to the poor man, "You stand there" or "Sit on the floor by my feet,"* [4] *have you not discriminated among yourselves and become judges with evil thoughts?*
>
> [5] **Listen, my dear brothers and sisters: Has not God chosen those who are poor in the eyes of the world to be rich in faith and to inherit the kingdom he promised those who love him?** [6] *But you have dishonored the poor. Is it not the rich who are exploiting you? Are they not*

the ones who are dragging you into court? [7] Are they not the ones who are blaspheming the noble name of him to whom you belong?

[8] If you really keep the royal law found in Scripture, "Love your neighbor as yourself," you are doing right. [9] But if you show favoritism, you sin and are convicted by the law as lawbreakers.

The passages we have already read in Mathew 6 and Revelation 2, all, in one way or another, speak of walking in obedience, mercy, kindness, and giving to the poor and those who can't pay you back. All these are counted as ways to put your treasure in heaven.

CHAPTER 4

INVESTING IN ETERNITY PAYS HIGHER INTEREST THAN HOARDING WEALTH HERE

Since I have just talked about what spiritual riches truly are, I thought this would be a good place to build on that and also correct some misuse of scripture. In addition, I want to make a further analogy to the contrast of gaining and consuming wealth here on earth versus opening a heavenly bank account where (since we are talking about an eternity of benefits) one earns an incomprehensible rate of return. One of many ways to invest in this heavenly bank account to earn this astronomical rate of return, is to help the truly poor and needy, especially poor believers.

The scripture I will discuss shortly, was not written to discuss a collection for a church general fund offering of any kind. It was a collection only for the believers who were having the hardest time in those days, those in Jerusalem and that vicinity. Prosperity preachers, however, take some of the verses out of context for their twisted reasons without explanation as to the true purpose of these passages. Even non-prosperity preachers "borrow" some of these verses on giving to the poor for their regular church (general fund) offerings and the regular church member thinks these passages are talking about giving to the church or a ministry in general and not about taking up a collection for the poor, because that is how they are presented.

I think that even though there probably are some appropriate applications of the same principles here in giving to the poor and in giving to the church for other reasons, I think it is much more honest if ministers explain the true context of the verses. I believe the congregations of most churches want to support their church anyway, so why not just be completely honest with them.

During Paul's time, many of the Jews in Jerusalem who were followers of Jesus, had their possessions taken away from them because of following Christ. Others were killed or placed in prison and their families suffered. Paul himself was a leader in some of this persecution before he was saved. Gentile converts to Christianity who were doing alright financially and who learned of the plight of these poor, had a God given desire to help their brothers and sisters in Christ. Some of the gentile believers, the ones in Macedonia, were in poverty themselves, but still wanted to help and Paul gives high praise to them for the desire to give and for the following-through, as well. I want to detail how preachers misuse some of these passages and explain what the truth of the situation was. This collection for the poor is discussed in Rom. 15:25-28; I Cor. 16:1-4, and II Cor. chapters 8 & 9. Luke also quotes Paul, in Acts 24:17, as saying he came back to Jerusalem to deliver this offering. I quote the main passages about this collection so there will be no doubt what Paul was discussing.

I start with First Corinthians 16:1-4:

> *Now about the collection for the Lord's people: Do what I told the Galatian churches to do. ² On the first day of every week, each one of you should set aside a sum of money in keeping with your income, saving it up, so that when I come no collections will have to be made. ³ Then, when I arrive, I will give letters of introduction to the men you approve and send them with your gift to Jerusalem. ⁴ If it seems advisable for me to go also, they will accompany me.*

These words are self-evident in their meaning. Paul writes to this church a second time right before he comes to receive what they collected, in his second epistle to the Corinthians. I will start with chapter 8:1-9:

> *And now, brothers and sisters, we want you to know about the grace that God has given the Macedonian churches. ² In the midst of a very severe trial, their overflowing joy and their extreme poverty welled up in rich generosity. ³ For I testify that they gave as much as they were able, and even beyond their ability. Entirely on their own, ⁴ they urgently pleaded with us for the privilege of sharing in this service to the Lord's people. ⁵ And they exceeded our expectations: They gave themselves first of all to the Lord, and then by the will of God also to us. ⁶ So we urged Titus, just as he had earlier made a beginning, to bring also to completion this act of grace on your part. ⁷ But since you excel in everything—in faith, in speech, in knowledge, in complete earnestness and in the love we have kindled in you—see that you also excel in this grace of giving.*
>
> *⁸ I am not commanding you, but I want to test the sincerity of your love by comparing it with the earnestness of others.* **⁹ For you know the grace of our Lord Jesus Christ, that though he was rich, yet for your sake he became poor, so that you through his poverty might become rich.**

I will address verse 9 in a moment, but first, the *"rich generosity"* he mentions in vs. 2 is something God puts in the hearts of believers when it comes to loving their fellow man, and especially loving fellow Christians. I believe where Paul says "they gave themselves first of all to the Lord," implies they prayed over what they were to give and probably asked God to help them to provide their best offering because they knew the difficulty of their fellow believers.

I put verse nine in bold print because this is a verse the prosperity teachers/preachers like to use to prove to their listeners and readers that

Christians can and should be rich. Paul, however, in the same book, written just a little before this, in chapter 5 verses 14-15:

> For Christ's love compels us, because we are convinced that Christ died for all, and therefore all died. And he died for all, _that those who live should no longer live for themselves but for him who died for them and was raised again._

The same Apostle Paul who wrote II Cor. 8:9, also wrote I Timothy 6:3-11, parts of which I have used already in this book. Let's compare it with those verses.

> [3] _If anyone teaches otherwise and does not agree to the sound instruction of our Lord Jesus Christ and to godly teaching,_ [4] _they are conceited and understand nothing. They have an unhealthy interest in controversies and quarrels about words that result in envy, strife, malicious talk, evil suspicions_ [5] **and constant friction between people of corrupt mind, who have been robbed of the truth and who think that godliness is a means to financial gain.**

> [6] **But godliness with contentment is great gain.** [7] _For we brought nothing into the world, and we can take nothing out of it._ [8] _But if we have food and clothing, we will be content with that._ [9] _Those who want to get rich fall into temptation and a trap and into many foolish and harmful desires that plunge people into ruin and destruction._ [10] _For the love of money is a root of all kinds of evil. Some people, eager for money, have wandered from the faith and pierced themselves with many griefs._

> [11] _But you, man of God, flee from all this, and pursue righteousness, godliness, faith, love, endurance and gentleness._

First of all, I know that Paul writes some things that, as Peter said, are hard to understand and these passages are certainly some of them. See the quote from II Peter 3:16:

> [16] *He writes the same way in all his letters, speaking in them of these matters. His letters contain some things that are hard to understand, which ignorant and unstable people distort, as they do the other Scriptures, to their own destruction.*

I believe the prosperity preachers/teachers, among others, are people who distort the Word, to their own destruction.

The principle of "paradoxical truth" that I discuss in the Appendix and elsewhere, is part of what is needed to understand this seeming contradiction. A paradoxical truth is where God shines the light of different conditions on a topic and shows different aspects of an issue, so we can understand in more detail a doctrine or principle. A paradoxical truth is one that seems to be contradictive, but is not. As an example, "more haste, less speed" is a paradox. As we have already seen, there are different kinds of riches, and prosperity preachers are eager to ignore that fact and misuse scripture talking about spiritual riches.

Also, we can use the "weight of scripture" principle here, that is, we look at how many scripture verses in the Word promote the gaining of financial riches on earth and how many do not. How many verses promote heavenly or "spiritual" riches? And, what does the Bible teach are true riches? What kind of riches was Paul speaking of in II Corinthians 8:9? You have already read many Bible verses that cover the different types of wealth and many verses that warn about trusting in money. You will read many more before you finish this book so you can decide for yourself where the balance of the Word lies on this doctrine.

See verse 6 in the last passage, *"godliness with contentment is great gain."* You might say that "great gain" is riches. Also notice back in II Cor. 8:1-9 that there were very poor believers (those in Jerusalem) and some that were a little better off (the Macedonians), though still in poverty, and some who were doing alright (the Corinthians). **So, when prosperity preachers use verse 9 of that chapter to say Christians** can and should be rich on earth, they are leaving out two thirds of the Christians in that larger passage who were neither rich nor even doing fairly well.

Also, regarding taking the whole of scripture into account when we discuss a particular doctrine, remember what Jesus says in Matthew 6:19-21:

> [19] *"Do not store up for yourselves treasures on earth, where moths and vermin destroy, and where thieves break in and steal.* [20] *But store up for yourselves treasures in heaven, where moths and vermin do not destroy, and where thieves do not break in and steal.* [21] *For where your treasure is, there your heart will be also.*

I hope you are seeing how prosperity preachers are good at picking and choosing just the verses that promote their agenda (raising money for themselves) and ignore verses that contradict their agenda. Returning to my analogy of the "fake news" and the reporters that just present information and misinformation that promotes their agendas, these false prophets that promote the prosperity message, ignore scripture that contradicts their goal and often twist out of context the verses they do use.

Going back to the quoting of II Cor. 8, the next six verses (10-15) bring out very valuable principles for ministers to remember regarding giving. That is, that the desire to give is what is important and God cares about equality of material possessions, at least equality in essentials, and probably more. I may have made some of you pause with that statement about equality of possessions. I am not a socialist by any means, but the love of God in our hearts does draw us to share with those truly in need, especially Christians in need. I say "truly in need," because there are those who are poor because of making bad choices on a regular basis, to include just being lazy, and if you give money to them, they will make more bad choices with what they receive. In which case, you might be funding their next drug trip or drinking binge. I am not talking about doing that at all and there always needs to be discretion used when giving to anyone or any group. Remember that Paul also wrote, *"He who will not work, shall not eat,"* (II Thessalonians 3:10). This is not being cruel, but using what some call tough love. In counseling, I advise people that if they do something for someone else that the person can and should be doing for themselves, they are not helping them, they are just enabling lazy/dependent behavior.

Here are those next six verses of II Cor. 8:

> [10] *And here is my judgment about what is best for you in this matter. Last year you were the first not only to give but also to have the desire to do so.* [11] *Now finish the work, so that your eager willingness to do it may be matched by your completion of it, **according to your means.*** [12] ***For if the willingness is there, the gift is acceptable according to what one has, not according to what one does not have.***

> [13] *Our desire is not that others might be relieved while you are hard pressed, but that there might be equality.* [14] *At the present time your plenty will supply what they need, so that in turn their plenty will supply what you need. The goal is equality,* [15] *as it is written: "The one who gathered much did not have too much, and the one who gathered little did not have too little."*

Verses 13-15 in the preceding text, teach us that when a believer does have financial resources they can spare to share, then they should pray over helping their brothers who are truly in need. This is practicing the love of God (see I John 4). I believe it is also storing away treasure in heaven. If we do not have this love in our hearts, we should seriously question our salvation. As Paul points out in the preceding passage, we might be the next one who needs help and then the shoe may be on the other foot and someone else may have to help us. Paul continues to write to the Corinthians about the details of who will be coming to receive the gift and about related things, in chapter 8:16 through 9:5. You can look up that passage and read it on your own if you want to.

Fortunately for Americans, generally speaking we have been in a good position financially to be among those who can share with Christians in need around the world and with some in our own communities as well. Thankfully, we have done that fairly well. Let's look at some of these other "giving to the poor" verses preachers use, beginning with II Cor. 9:6-8. I will put in bold the passages most used.

> **⁶ Remember this: Whoever sows sparingly will also reap sparingly, and whoever sows generously will also reap generously.**

> ⁷ Each of you should give what you have decided in your heart to give, not reluctantly or under compulsion, for **God loves a cheerful giver. ⁸ And God is able to bless you abundantly, so that in all things at all times, having all that you need, you will abound in every good work.**

They usually do not read most of verse seven so I did not highlight it. That kind of conflicts with the compulsion many ministers want to promote. Please see that verse eight says *"having all that you need, you will abound in every good work."* You see that Paul is saying to the Corinthians that God will bless them abundantly, not so they can consume it on their lusts, but rather, so they can have all they need to do God's will in their lives.

They also do not usually discuss verse nine:

> ⁹ *As it is written:*
> *"They have freely scattered their gifts to the poor;*
> *their righteousness endures forever."*

Some preachers also like to use the next two verses because they can be used to promote giving to the general fund and can be used to some degree to appeal to greed:

> ¹⁰ *Now he who supplies seed to the sower and bread for food will also supply and increase your store of seed and will enlarge the harvest of your righteousness.*

¹¹ You will be enriched in every way so that you can be generous on every occasion, and through us your generosity will result in thanksgiving to God.

Even though these verses can be used the wrong way, please notice <u>again</u> what the emphasis really is here. You are not being given things so you can hoard wealth, but so you can be "generous on every occasion." So, God does not help people to prosper financially without expecting them to share that prosperity with others, even to the point of their being equality for the truly needy. If a non-prosperity teaching minister explains that and explains that the verses were originally used for a collection for the poor, then I don't think there is anything wrong with using these passages during an offering for the general fund. Notice also, in verse ten it says "enlarge the harvest of your righteousness." The emphasis there is not on financial benefits. Why then, do so many financial prosperity teachers hoard wealth and still keep asking for more and more money? Why do they keep encouraging believers to pursue riches and to accumulate wealth here on earth? I think it is because wolves are never satisfied. Their sowing and reaping messages, their "seed faith" schemes, make it sound like they are doing you a favor by taking more and more of your money so you can get more and more for yourself. They remind me of modern day "Carny's" or carnival hawkers; they are like the old medicine show patent medicine "snake oil" salesmen. They paint a pretty picture, but like the "cupie" doll worth $1 that cost you $20 to win, you will be throwing your money away basically, if you fall for their schemes.

As I have discussed, financially well-off people then, have a responsibility to share with those in need, not to use wealth to think of themselves as being better than the poor, or to "consume it upon their own lusts," but to share when the right opportunity is there. This type of giving can also be a ministry and evangelistic tool for third world countries where giving not only helps spread the gospel, but provides poor believers with a healthier way to live, like having clean water wells perhaps, and some needed education for themselves and their children… you know, things God wants them to have and for which he may have helped you have extra money so you could contribute.

In so doing, God is truly giving you an opportunity to put up treasure for yourself in heaven while helping others. Remember that scripture says it is more blessed to give than to receive (Acts: 20:35). This providing for the poor is one way money can help you earn spiritual riches. Plus, you feel great about yourself and happy inside when you know you have followed the leading of the Holy Spirit and used your extra money in such a way. You also get to share the joy of the people who receive your gift. The recipients of your gift truly know that the love of God is in others and it witnesses to them about how good God is, so it truly results in praises to God.

So, you get joy, peace of mind, and treasure in heaven. What a deal! It makes me want to pray more about where God wants me to contribute next, so I can get blessed (in the right ways). That is a win, win, win. I want that kind of riches. God gives us what we need to really do his will and be blessed more than we can even imagine, not with things that waste away, but with eternal blessings.

Verses 12-15 of chapter nine of II Corinthians complete Paul's statements of appreciation to the givers and his thanksgiving to God as well.

> *12 This service that you perform is not only supplying the needs of the Lord's people but is also overflowing in many expressions of thanks to God. 13 Because of the service by which you have proved yourselves, others will praise God for the obedience that accompanies your confession of the gospel of Christ, and for your generosity in sharing with them and with everyone else. 14 And in their prayers for you their hearts will go out to you, because of the surpassing grace God has given you. 15 Thanks be to God for his indescribable gift!*

Paul wrote the following after he had made this collection; Romans 15:25-28 says:

> *25 Now, however, I am on my way to Jerusalem in the service of the Lord's people there. 26 For Macedonia and*

Achaia were pleased to make a contribution for the poor among the Lord's people in Jerusalem. ²⁷ They were pleased to do it, and indeed they owe it to them. For if the Gentiles have shared in the Jews' spiritual blessings, they owe it to the Jews to share with them their material blessings. ²⁸ So after I have completed this task and have made sure that they have received this contribution, I will go to Spain and visit you on the way.

Paul was a very cool guy and he is certainly one person I want to see when I get to heaven. It will probably be a long line for that privilege, but worth it. The Bible really does have a lot in it about helping the poor and I cover more when I get to the chapter about tithing.

CHAPTER 5

BIBLE STATEMENTS ABOUT WEALTH BEING A POTENTIAL PROBLEM

The Bible also speaks much about wealth being a potential problem and an impediment to spiritual growth rather than an asset! I will list some of these soon. As I have been saying, true success and prosperity is found in being in the perfect will of God at whatever point in your life you find yourself. The Apostle Paul said he had learned the secret of being content in whatever situation he was in, whether in want or in plenty.

Philippians 4:10-13:

> [10] *I rejoiced greatly in the Lord that at last you renewed your concern for me. Indeed, you were concerned, but you had no opportunity to show it.* [11] *I am not saying this because I am in need, for I have learned to be content whatever the circumstances.* [12] *I know what it is to be in need, and I know what it is to have plenty. I have learned the secret of being content in any and every situation, whether well fed or hungry, whether living in plenty or*

in want. ¹³ I can do all this through him who gives me strength.

Frankly, none of the apostles ever had any significant worldly wealth but, were all rich in faith and in good deeds and in being obedient to Christ. Peter talks about what he thought being a good shepherd of a flock was like:

1 Peter 5:1-4:

> *To the elders among you, I appeal as a fellow elder and a witness of Christ's sufferings who also will share in the glory to be revealed: ² Be shepherds of God's flock that is under your care, watching over them—not because you must, but because you are willing, as God wants you to be;* **not pursuing dishonest gain, but eager to serve;** *³ not lording it over those entrusted to you, but being examples to the flock. ⁴ And when the Chief Shepherd appears, you will receive the crown of glory that will never fade away.*

As I have already stated, there is also the account of the rich young ruler who was told by Jesus to go and sell all he had and give it to the poor. He rejected this and went away sad. I quote the actual verses here. When you read it, pay particular attention to what Jesus says about rich people going to heaven in verses 24-25.

Luke 18:18-25:

> *¹⁸ A certain ruler asked him, "Good teacher, what must I do to inherit eternal life?"*
>
> *¹⁹ "Why do you call me good?" Jesus answered. "No one is good—except God alone. ²⁰ You know the commandments: 'You shall not commit adultery, you shall not murder, you shall not steal, you shall not give false testimony, honor your father and mother.'"*

²¹ "All these I have kept since I was a boy," he said.

²² When Jesus heard this, he said to him, "You still lack one thing. Sell everything you have and give to the poor, and you will have treasure in heaven. Then come, follow me."

²³ When he heard this, he became very sad, because he was very wealthy. **²⁴ Jesus looked at him and said, "How hard it is for the rich to enter the kingdom of God! ²⁵ Indeed, it is easier for a camel to go through the eye of a needle than for someone who is rich to enter the kingdom of God."**

A camel going through the eye of a needle was a well-known thing to the people of that time. It was not impossible, as it would be with a sewing needle. An eye of the needle referred to a tax gate which camels laden with trade goods would have to pass through before they could enter a city. This meant that all of the goods loaded on the camel had to be removed and checked so they could be taxed before going into a city to be sold. After they were taxed, they could be loaded back onto the camel for carrying. The analogy is plain. Rich people may have a lot of worldly wealth, but not one bit of it goes with them, nor does it buy them anything once they get there. Indeed, they are admonished by scripture not to trust in their wealth. This man refused to give up worldly wealth and instead gave up heavenly treasure that would have lasted forever. Going by what they say today, the so-called faith/prosperity teachers would have said Jesus had it wrong. They would have said something like "If the poor just had faith, they would not be poor." The prosperity teachers would have, and still do, miss out on the main way to have lasting riches, because they almost always focus on having temporary riches that fade away.

Other Bible passages continue this theme. Please read the following passages, especially those in bold print.

Luke 6:20-26:

²⁰ Looking at his disciples, he said:
"Blessed are you who are poor,

for yours is the kingdom of God.
[21] Blessed are you who hunger now,
for you will be satisfied.
Blessed are you who weep now,
for you will laugh.
[22] Blessed are you when people hate you,
when they exclude you and insult you
and reject your name as evil,
because of the Son of Man.
[23] "Rejoice in that day and leap for joy,
because great is your reward in heaven. For that is how
their ancestors treated the prophets.
[24] "But woe to you who are rich,
for you have already received your comfort.
[25] Woe to you who are well fed now,
for you will go hungry.
Woe to you who laugh now,
for you will mourn and weep.
[26] Woe to you when everyone speaks well of you,
for that is how their ancestors treated the false prophets.

Matthew 6:24:

> *[24] "No one can serve two masters. Either you will hate*
> *the one and love the other, or you will be devoted to the*
> *one and despise the other. You cannot serve both God*
> *and money.*

The story of Lazarus and the rich man in Luke gives us a warning for the rich to not trust in their wealth alone.

Luke 16:19-25:

> *[19] "There was a rich man who was dressed in purple and*
> *fine linen and lived in luxury every day. [20] At his gate was*
> *laid a beggar named Lazarus, covered with sores [21] and*

longing to eat what fell from the rich man's table. Even the dogs came and licked his sores.

[22] "The time came when the beggar died and the angels carried him to Abraham's side. The rich man also died and was buried. [23] In Hades, where he was in torment, he looked up and saw Abraham far away, with Lazarus by his side. [24] So he called to him, 'Father Abraham, have pity on me and send Lazarus to dip the tip of his finger in water and cool my tongue, because I am in agony in this fire.'

[25] "But Abraham replied, 'Son, remember that in your lifetime you received your good things, while Lazarus received bad things, but now he is comforted here and you are in agony.

It should be noted that you can also wind up with a twisted version of the Bible by teaching one doctrine in a balanced way, but excluding most other doctrines in your teaching, such as teaching mostly about the benefits of being a Christian without teaching the responsibilities of it. The truth is that the more responsible, obedient, and self-disciplined a Christian is, the more benefits he/she will probably have in Christ in this life, but he/she will especially have them in the next life. Indeed, every good promise in the Bible is conditional. I will repeat that. **Every good promise in the Bible is conditional**. Likewise, every promise of punishment is conditional. God does not bless bad behavior nor punish good behavior.

We have to know the whole truth about God's teaching in order to recognize lies. We have to see how all the parts of the truth fit together to understand how the truth works. Here are some more "rich person" passages that seem to go along with the Lazarus/rich man passage, first from the New Testament, then from the Old:

James 5:1-3:

> *Now listen, you rich people, weep and wail because of the misery that is coming on you.* ² *Your wealth has rotted, and moths have eaten your clothes.*³ *Your gold and silver are corroded. Their corrosion will testify against you and eat your flesh like fire. You have hoarded wealth in the last days.*

Luke 1:53:

> ⁵³ *He has filled the hungry with good things but has sent the rich away empty.*

Jeremiah 9:23:

> ²³ *This is what the* Lord *says:* *"Let not the wise boast of their wisdom or the strong boast of their strength or the rich boast of their riches,*

I bet most of the readers of this book did not realize before now, just how many negative things there were in the Bible aimed at rich people or riches.

BIBLICAL PRINCIPLES <u>CAN</u> LEAD TO FINANCIAL AS WELL AS SPIRITUAL SUCCESS

It is true that the Bible teaches us to be hard workers, to be diligent, to use wisdom, to be responsible, and to use the abilities we have to do our best at whatever we do, even as if we were working for Christ, because that is what we are doing.

Colossians 3:23-24:

> ²³ *Whatever you do, work at it with all your heart, as working for the Lord, not for human masters,* ²⁴ *since you*

know that you will receive an inheritance from the Lord
as a reward. It is the Lord Christ you are serving.

Ecclesiastes 9:10 is a similar passage to that one. The Bible also teaches us to take care of our bodies and not to get drunk or to do anything in excess. Also, the fruits of the Spirit are attributes every believer should have in increasing measure.

Galatians 5:22-23:

[22] *But the fruit of the Spirit is love, joy, peace, forbearance, kindness, goodness, faithfulness,* [23] *gentleness and self-control. Against such things there is no law.*

As already stated, believers are to be hard workers. What employer does not want to hire, to train, and to promote hard workers who also are kind, faithful, gentle, and have self-control, when he or she can? This is a main reason why, in the religious freedom we still (for now at least) enjoy in America, devout believers who are mature in Christ have tended to achieve above average success in whatever field they chose to pursue. This usually results in financial rewards. It is also true that we should give responsibly, according to our means, and not withhold unduly in our giving and this involves more than just giving money or possessions. It also involves giving time and energy, work and care.

The following verses were just quoted in the previous chapter. I should remind the reader that these lines were written to discuss a collection for the poor and not for a regular church offering. That said, I do think these and the other verses used here apply in any worthwhile area of Christian giving, as long as their true context is explained. I quote them again here because they are basically very positive scriptures and because I want to contrast them with some "spinach" type scripture on the same issue so the reader can see a balance.

2 Corinthians. 9:6-11:

[6] *Remember this: Whoever sows sparingly will also reap sparingly, and whoever sows generously will also reap*

generously. ⁷ Each of you should give what you have decided in your heart to give, not reluctantly or under compulsion, for God loves a cheerful giver. ⁸ And God is able to bless you abundantly, so that in all things at all times, having all that you need, you will abound in every good work. ⁹ As it is written:

"They have freely scattered their gifts to the poor; their righteousness endures forever."

¹⁰ Now he who supplies seed to the sower and bread for food will also supply and increase your store of seed and will enlarge the harvest of your righteousness. ¹¹ You will be enriched in every way so that you can be generous on every occasion, and through us your generosity will result in thanksgiving to God.

These are encouraging statements for the most part, but, as I wrote in the last chapter, the people for whom this collection was being made, were not doing well and there are times when being a Christian who lives what he/she believes produces a negative response in their finances and career opportunities generally speaking, as in the case of the believers in Jerusalem that received the gift Paul and others collected. Paul writes about this difficulty/hardship type of thing in his own life when he wrote to Timothy in the following verses:

2 Timothy 3:10-12:

¹⁰ You, however, know all about my teaching, my way of life, my purpose, faith, patience, love, endurance, ¹¹ persecutions, sufferings—what kinds of things happened to me in Antioch, Iconium and Lystra, the persecutions I endured. Yet the Lord rescued me from all of them. ¹² In fact, <u>everyone who wants to live a godly life in Christ Jesus will be persecuted,</u>

You don't hear the "fake faith" preachers spending much time on those last verses do you? As stated, they remind me of the corrupt politicians and "fake news" broadcasters who spin everything that does not agree with their agendas to seem very different than it actually is. For instance, these preachers criticize anyone who went through trials as a believer, as just not having had enough faith. Thus Paul, Job, Jeremiah, and an innumerable multitude of other believers, whose sandals the "fake faith" preachers are not fit to untie, are said to be lacking in faith.

In probably the best chapter in the Bible on examples of faith, Hebrews 11, the author writes about many people who received from God what they needed to be victorious in their service to God (not in self-serving consuming) and it all sounds uplifting until you get to the second part of verse 35 then you notice a change. I will quote verses 35-40:

Hebrews 11:35-40:

> [35] *Women received back their dead, raised to life again. There were others who were tortured, refusing to be released so that they might gain an even better resurrection.* [36] *Some faced jeers and flogging, and even chains and imprisonment.* [37] *They were put to death by stoning; they were sawed in two; they were killed by the sword. They went about in sheepskins and goatskins, destitute, persecuted and mistreated—* [38] *the world was not worthy of them. They wandered in deserts and mountains, living in caves and in holes in the ground.*
>
> [39] *These were all commended for their faith, yet none of them received what had been promised,* [40] *since God had planned something better for us so that only together with us would they be made perfect.*

These passages show different aspects of faith. Just as Paul wrote to the Corinthians about a situation in his life, sometimes we get what we pray for and sometimes God has other plans:

II Corinthians 12:8-10:

> [8] *Three times I pleaded with the Lord to take it away from me.* [9] *But he said to me, "My grace is sufficient for you, for my power is made perfect in weakness." Therefore, I will boast all the more gladly about my weaknesses, so that Christ's power may rest on me.* [10] *That is why, for Christ's sake, I delight in weaknesses, in insults, in hardships, in persecutions, in difficulties. For when I am weak, then I am strong.*

Since all God's Word is true, then all scripture must be taken in balance, allowing for the influences of covenant, content, and context. We also must consider the weight of scripture principle; again, that is, how much of the Bible seems to be saying one thing about a topic in scripture and how much of it seems to be saying something quite different. We must consider: who is speaking, what is he or she saying, and how does it apply to us as believers today. So, no preacher or Bible teacher should ever just pick a few verses out and make a doctrine out of it without considering what the rest of the Bible has to say on that subject. For more clarity on these interpretation factors, please read or review the Appendix.

It seems the whole book of I Peter deals with the suffering of Christ first, then of the suffering of us his servants. The following passages are notable: 2:19-23; 4:15-19.

I Peter 2:19-23:

> [19] *For it is commendable if someone bears up under the pain of unjust suffering because they are conscious of God.* [20] *But how is it to your credit if you receive a beating for doing wrong and endure it? But if you suffer for doing good and you endure it, this is commendable before God.* [21] *To this you were called, because Christ suffered for you, leaving you an example, that you should follow in his steps.*

[22] *"He committed no sin,*
and no deceit was found in his mouth."
[23] *When they hurled their insults at him, he did not*
retaliate; when he suffered, he made no threats. Instead,
he entrusted himself to him who judges justly.

I Peter 4:15-19:

[15] *If you suffer, it should not be as a murderer or thief*
or any other kind of criminal, or even as a meddler. *[16]*
However, if you suffer as a Christian, do not be ashamed,
but praise God that you bear that name. *[17]* *For it is time*
for judgment to begin with God's household; and if it
begins with us, what will the outcome be for those who
do not obey the gospel of God? *[18]* *And,*

"If it is hard for the righteous to be saved,
what will become of the ungodly and the sinner?"
[19] *So then, those who suffer according to God's will,*
should commit themselves to their faithful Creator and
continue to do good.

I remember years ago when I worked at a union manufacturing job. I ran a "spot welder" machine that was old and hard to run. The four machines the company had were labeled A-D. My machine was "D," which the employees nicknamed "Dog machine" due to being so hard to run. When I first got the promotion from laborer to machine operator, I inherited the least popular machine of course. All the operators had convinced the foremen that you could not make the hourly rate of production on "Dog," so the foremen just did not expect as much from it. After I took over, it was about three or four months before I had it making production. I had my life threatened by some of those union members because I moved the bar for them as well and set a higher standard of work. I called their bluff, however, and am glad to say they did not try anything physical.

On the same job I was threatened for tearing down some nude

pictures one or two of the workers had taped up in the bathroom one day. Two of the workers threatened me over that, but I reported the threat to management and the workers did nothing. As Christians in Syria, Iraq, and other places in recent years have found out, standing up for Christ can cost you torture or even your life. Christians in communist countries have known this for many decades.

So, how does all this scripture and discussion match with what the prosperity preachers teach? I remember in the 1970's when all of this started gaining steam, there was one style of teaching that most non-denominational Charismatic or Full-Gospel preachers were using to promote the promises of God. It went something like: If you do this, this, and this, God **has** to do this, this, and this. They said it was a law, that if you did a particular thing, God had to do whatever (fill in the blank). There is a little truth in this, especially regarding salvation but, it was taken way overboard. I was young in years and lacked knowledge in scripture and in the principles of God at the time and went along with it for a while, but after a few years, I came to the conclusion that God does not have to do anything but be faithful to his principles; that we presume way too much about what God wants for us and what is really best for us and many of our wants and desires are either contrary to God's will and/or are just not in our own best interest nor in the best interest of the Kingdom of God.

Because God does care for us, he does not give us many of the foolish things we ask for. He will be true to himself, however, and act on his principles. It is then, his principles, his "ways" that he will keep. We can make up all the rules we want to and say he has to keep them, but I am convinced God is not someone we can manipulate. Unlike the title of Kenneth Hagin's book "You Can Have What You Say!" implies, we do not dictate to him and he is not bound by what we tell or ask him to do, unless we are praying for what we know is his will and nothing more, and we leave room for his discretion and adjustments. When God answers our prayers, it will always be in accordance with his ways, that is, his principles. In counseling we learn to ask "open ended" questions of clients so they can go in the direction they want with their answer. It makes sense likewise, to pray "open ended" prayers that have the general item requested that we believe we need, but that asks God to please answer the prayer in the manner he thinks best. God knows ahead of time what we need and He does not need us to dictate to him the details about what is best for us. It is foolishness on our part, if we do.

This reminds me of the country music song "Unanswered Prayers," written and sung by Garth Brooks back in 1990. Pull it up on YouTube if you don't know it.

In the first two lines, Brooks says:

> Just the other night at a hometown football game
> My wife and I ran into my old highschool flame

He goes on to tell about how much he had loved and wanted that girl to be his wife and how he had prayed every night for God to bring that about. Seeing her now though, after many years and learning about the person she had become, and looking at her compared to his wife, he was very grateful that God had not answered his many heartfelt prayers. He finishes the song by singing:

> Sometimes I thank God for unanswered prayers
> Remember when you're talkin' to the man upstairs
> That just because he may not answer doesn't mean he don't care
> Some of God's greatest gifts are unanswered
>
> Some of God's greatest gifts are all too often unanswered…
> Some of God's greatest gifts are unanswered prayers

We need to be praying for God to guide us in His will and to provide us with the things we need that will help us to do His will. We should not be praying for God to provide for our self-will, even if it includes what we consider to be "good works."

I wrote a little poem in the late 70's that expressed my thinking at the time because God just wasn't doing what I wanted Him to do:

I do not know the mind of God,
He won't get in my box.
I try to bind Him in my mold,
But He just breaks the stocks.

I believe I know more of the mind of God today than I did back then,
and I know we are told in I Cor. 2 that we can have the mind of Christ,
but this is acquired by humbly and patiently seeking his will and getting
on board with him, not by us deciding what we want to have and what
we want to do, and getting God onboard with us.

CHAPTER

THE TRUTH ABOUT THE "HUNDRED-FOLD" TEACHING

O ne of the most abused verses of the "Ponzi scheme," "get rich quick if you have enough faith," part of the so-called prosperity message is about getting a hundred times what you have given:

Mark 10:28-30:

> [28] Then Peter spoke up, "We have left everything to follow you!"
>
> [29] "Truly I tell you," Jesus replied, "no one who has left home or brothers or sisters or mother or father or children or fields for me and the gospel [30] will fail to receive a hundred times as much in this present age: homes, brothers, sisters, mothers, children and fields—along with persecutions—and in the age to come eternal life.

Now, let me just ask a few rhetorical questions here that have apparent answers. If we leave our brothers and/or sisters for Christ, is our physical mother really going to get pregnant another one or two or three hundred (depending on how many siblings we have) more times and produce more brothers and sisters in volume for us? If we have left our physical parents for Christ, is there any physical way we can get more? Have you ever known a Christian who gave away a home or other property as a donation to a ministry and over the next ten or however many years received a hundred houses or fields? I have not. So, was Jesus lying or was he talking about a different kind of return? I think it was the latter.

When a person becomes a Christian they truly do walk away from their old lives in many ways and they certainly may give up friends and relatives who are not and who do not choose to become Christians. However, I do not just have a hundred brothers to replace the one I gave up because he chose a different religion, I have thousands of them in Christ. If I go to almost any city in this country and in most major cities of the world in service to Christ, there I will find a body of believers who will look after me for a while just like a family would because we are family. They are my brothers, sisters, and mothers and fathers in Christ. I would not lack a home to stay in if I needed a place to stay. When there is a legitimate need a minister has, God moves upon the hearts of other believers to meet that need. I have left fairly good job situations because I truly felt God was leading me to go in a different direction as part of his plan for my life. In this modern-day life, that was the equivalent of giving up my field if I was a farmer or giving up my fishing boat if I was a fisherman like Peter. Peter became a fisher of men and caught souls instead of flounders. Which sea do you think Peter would rather have fished? Others left their fields and became workers in God's harvest fields. Which fields do you think they valued more? But these are just the good things we receive for our service in the kingdom. There are difficulties as well and the so-called prosperity teachers/preachers ignore that last part of verse 30 I quoted, which says "and persecutions."

If these fake faith preachers say you are to get literally a hundred times of what you gave, then you will receive lots, and lots of persecutions too, I guess. And will somebody please tell me where in those verses does it mention money? I believe Jesus said nothing about money here because he was talking about if a person gives him their life, they will get it back <u>a hundred times more full</u>. They will find out what family really is, what fulfillment really is, what love really is, and what true riches are. At the beginning of that journey they will also find eternal life. I believe this was part of what Paul wrote about in the following verses:

Philippians 3:7-9:

> [7] *But whatever were gains to me I now consider loss for the sake of Christ.* [8] *What is more, I consider everything a loss because of the surpassing worth of knowing Christ Jesus my Lord, for whose sake I have lost all things. I consider them garbage, that I may gain Christ* [9] *and be found in him, not having a righteousness of my own that comes from the law, but that which is through faith in Christ—the righteousness that comes from God on the basis of faith.*

Jesus Cleared the Temple of Money Changers Twice – So Much in the Bible Happens in Threes

Once at the beginning of his ministry (John 2:13-22) and again in the last week of his ministry (Mt. 21:12-17), Jesus got very angry, formed a whip and physically drove "money changers" out of his father's house (see also Mk. 11:17).

John 2:13-17:

> [13] *When it was almost time for the Jewish Passover, Jesus went up to Jerusalem.* [14] *In the temple courts he found people selling cattle, sheep and doves, and others sitting at tables exchanging money.* [15] *So he made a whip out of cords, and drove all from the temple courts, both sheep and cattle; he scattered the coins of the money changers and overturned their tables.* [16] *To those who sold doves he said, "Get these out of here! Stop turning my Father's house into a market!"* [17] *His disciples remembered that it is written: "Zeal for your house will consume me."*

Mt. 21:12-13:

> [12] *Jesus entered the temple courts and drove out all who were buying and selling there. He overturned the tables of the money changers and the benches of those selling doves.* [13] *"It is written," he said to them, "'My house will be called a house of prayer,' but you are making it 'a den of robbers.'"*

It seems that these "robbers" had figured out a way to milk the Jewish people out of money by using religious legalism and fraud. As the Mosaic (that given by Moses) law worship requirements directed, all of the Jewish males had to appear before the Lord at wherever the Tabernacle and later the Temple was, three times a year, to offer sacrifices and to have the Word taught to them by the priests. On Passover, which was part of the Feast of Unleavened Bread, a requirement was to offer a spotless lamb (Ex. 12:5 and Lev. 21:21). Each lamb had to be inspected by the priests before it was approved for sacrifice to show it was spotless, without blemish. The priests and other temple workers evidently, either ran a scheme or approved of others who ran it (probably getting a fee or percentage of profit) where nobody's lamb would be approved, and so you had to buy one of their "pre-approved" lambs at a highly inflated price. There were also times when a bull or pigeons were required, so those were covered too. Also, since Jewish people came from many different countries to worship at these feast/festival times, before they could purchase whatever animal they had to buy for sacrifice, they needed to exchange any currency not used in Israel, for that which was. This seems to have been done unfairly as well. Jesus was having none of this in his Father's house (Jer. 7:11) and he kicked them out. He had to do it the second time because they did not seem to get the message the first time. I believe he will do it again in one way or another because many religious people in our time have still not gotten the message.

Like the evil sons of the Priest Eli in I Samuel 2, these people in Jesus' time were bringing corruption and sin into God's house. God judged Hophni and Phinehas, Eli's sons, for they despised the Lord's offering, killing both them and their father on the same day. Eli was judged because he failed to discipline his sons, caring more for them than for God. I believe this so-called faith message, this so-called prosperity message has brought corruption into the church that parallels the worst offenses of the money changers of Jesus' time and the sins of Eli's sons. In some cases, I think it is as foolish and evil as Balaam, loving the wages from Barak instead of the provision of God. When Jesus comes to his dwelling, his church, again, I think he will be doing some spiritual house cleaning. I believe many of those who seem like big shots now will be among the least in the Kingdom of Heaven, if they are going in at all; while the poor that they ridiculed and discriminated against, will be some of the first. The pastors who are toiling in small congregations, but being faithful in shepherding their flock as God leads them and having to work at an outside job to make up for the support their flock could not provide (as Paul did) will, I believe, be some of the very first.

Matthew 20:16:

[16] *"So the last will be first, and the first will be last."*

As I have already written, it is shameful to me that most, if not all, of the prosperity preachers come from denominations or groups that believe in the baptism in the Holy Spirit as a second blessing after salvation. They come from groups that believe in the gifts of the Holy Spirit still being provided for the church today. To me, this means that they should have more discernment and insight into spiritual things than ministers from many "old line" non-Pentecostal, Christian denominations. But, Pentecostal or not, ministers from almost all, if not all denominations teach an extremely twisted version of what passes for Biblical tithing. It is nowhere near balanced or complete because it leaves the majority of verses on this subject out completely and thus puts meanings never meant onto the verses they do use.

Because the teaching of everyone giving a tenth to the church is such a major wide-spread teaching by so many ministers, of virtually every Christian group, it is a main topic in this book. However, before I go into that discussion, there is one more topic of a more general nature that I want to discuss. It also is important to help a believer become sound and balanced, one who is strong in his/her faith and able to refute error when it is encountered in churches. That is, we need to be able to deal with spiritual bullies who use their positional power, their titles, their degrees, and whatever else they can, to try to control the flock they are fleecing or otherwise treating in a false way. We must learn to set boundaries through use of the Word of God, which is the Sword of the Spirit, to deal powerfully with "bullies in the pulpit."

CHAPTER 7

BULLIES IN THE PULPIT AND HOW TO OVERCOME THEM

Almost everyone, if not everyone, has been bullied and nobody likes it. Some of us stand up to one degree or another to bullies, but it is not an easy thing to do. However, most physical bullies will back off to one degree or another if you stand up to them and let it be known you won't let them get away with it. There is another type of bully, which I call a psychological bully. Besides being a minister, I am a Licensed Professional Counselor, a LPC, so I know something about psychological bullying. Psychological bullies are somewhat different than the physical bully like "Butch" was on The Little Rascals. The games psychological bullies play (as in the book, Games People Play, by Eric Berne) are very fluid and they can change the script of the game to try to make themselves seem to be the victim and you the villain when you begin to stop tolerating any of their various forms of psychological abuse. Some people's relatives are great at this and are masters, it seems, at laying guilt trips on the people they want to control and manipulate. People of good will, who are kind in general, and who are perhaps a little passive, are easy targets for psychological abusers and at some point, will either have to learn to set healthy boundaries with their abusers or live a life of chaos and emotional pain. I have used a very good book on this in my counseling practice, simply called <u>Boundaries</u>, by Dr. Henry Cloud and Dr. John Townsend. It is subtitled, <u>When to Say Yes, How to Say No, To Take Control of Your Life</u>. It is sponsored by Zondervan Books and both authors are Christians.

Setting healthy boundaries is what is called in counseling, becoming assertive. An assertive person is not passive or aggressive. They are balanced in relationships and while they care about others, they also care about themselves. When I speak of a relationship here, I am not necessarily talking about a sexual relationship of any kind. It could be a friendship, or any type of adult family kinship. Unfortunately, I felt the need to clarify this because so many people think of unmarried people living together when you say the word "relationship." If you call yourself a Christian and are "shacking up" with somebody, you need to read I Corinthians 6:9 thru 7:9, and act appropriately on it.

Back on the topic of setting healthy boundaries, assertive people set boundaries with abusive people and require that the abusive person stop all forms of abuse toward them or the assertive person cuts off the relationship until they do comply with those boundaries. They demand that the relationship be fair, truthful, and healthy going both ways, or there not be a relationship. I believe this is what has to be done with some Bible teachers and preachers, who in my opinion, are spiritual bullies and who try to dominate and intimidate their followers into submission to doctrinal positions that scripture does not justify, but which benefit the preacher/teacher and/or their denomination. I believe these types of doctrines are what Jesus referred to as the "leaven of the Pharisees" (Matthew 16:6), when he told the disciples to beware of it. Of course, these bullies do not use physical intimidation. They don't flex their biceps or things like that, but they let you know in other ways that unless you want to be given the cold shoulder, shunned, embarrassed in front of the church, or even asked to leave the denomination you are in, you have to agree with them. In the same way, during the days of Jesus and of the apostles, people were thrown out of the synagogue by the Jewish leaders for accepting Jesus.

A major part of overcoming this type of bully is to realize that you don't need anything they have. If you are a Christian you already have fellowship with Christ and with God the Father and the Holy Spirit. So, as in the case of dealing with physical bullies in the school yard, a first step is to lose your fear of them. When you realize they don't have anything you actually need, or should even want, the leverage they have over you is virtually gone. You will have to leave your comfort zone perhaps, that doing what you are "used to" feeling, but if you are in such a position, it is time to move forward in your life with Christ and seek a purer, more truthful relationship both with God and in the body of Christ. Is God calling you out to begin some form of ministry yourself? Maybe God is just trying to get you into a body of believers whose walk and doctrine is closer to what you really believe. When God brought the children of Israel out of Egypt, Dt. 6:23 says he brought them out to bring them in – into the promised land. On the way, he taught them a pure form of worship (pure for the time). When God calls believers out of one place today, I believe it is to lead them into a better place. Entering the promised land of Israel was not without struggle. They had to fight to take it and to keep it, but the closer they stuck to the pure form of worship God gave them, the better they did in taking and keeping their land.

One option people who are dissatisfied with their current fellowship location may not have considered, is starting a house church. There is a growing move into house churches for many reasons. It only takes a few families or individuals to start a house church and there are house churches mentioned in scripture. The Apostle Paul writes about two of them; one in Rom. 16:3,5 and another in Col. 4:15. A minister named John Fenn has a ministry of leading and helping others start such churches. It is called, "Church Without Walls International." If you think God may be leading you into something like that, you can look up his ministry, among others, online. They provide guidance and connection for these groups. It does not matter how big or pretty the building is you worship in, it just matters how pure and true the worship that goes on inside is. In John 4:24 Jesus speaks about this.

> [24] *God is Spirit, and those who worship Him must worship in spirit and truth."*

Three times in the book of John, in Jn. 7:13; 9:22; and 12:42, it talks about people believing in Jesus as the Christ, but not saying anything about it because of fear of the Jews because the Jewish leaders had decided that anyone who accepted Jesus would be put out of the Synagogue (the equivalent of a church for us).

NEW FIRE

I remember in 1982, the then fiery young Baptist evangelist, James Robison, was speaking to the meeting of the Southern Baptist Convention in New Orleans and among other themes, he was openly ridiculing his own denomination for putting their traditions above the Word of God in their worship and teaching. Please understand that this can apply to almost any denomination and non-denominational group. I have an old tape of that sermon which I bought from the James Robison Evangelistic Association, Ft. Worth, Texas, back in 1982. The following excerpts are transcribed by me from that tape:

> "Some of you are saying, bless God I am going to go home and I am going to call for the Elders of the Church and I am going to anoint them (the sick) and they are going to get well. It's in the Word (James 5:13). Of course, don't dare do that. Not if you are a Baptist and want to keep your reputation as a Baptist. Don't dare anoint anybody with oil and pray for the sick. Even though God said do it. Just be careful now. **I MEAN, GOD SAID DO IT!** But we wouldn't want to do it now, would we? I mean it might taint our sterling reputation. Jesus said, "Beware the leaven of the Pharisees (Mt. 16:5-12)." Do you know what it (leaven of the Pharisees) is? It is the traditions of men taught as the commandments of God."

In another part of the sermon he said the following:

> "This (the Bible) is a war book. When it talks about sheep, it is talking about the people of God and when

it talks about the under shepherds it is talking about the ones God left behind to feed his flock and the only food his sheep can eat and get strong on is the Word of God. This (the Word) is the green pasture where you best be leading his flock or you are a false prophet. I don't care how many degrees you've got and I don't care how many positions you have held. This (the Word) is the food. And the Wolf and the Beast is the Devil ..."

James then quoted from Ezekiel 34:2 and 4 that, I have quoted before, but he used the KJV. I am listing my quotes in the NIV to keep my Bible referencing easier. Feel free to look at it in the KJV if you wish:

> [2] *"Son of man, prophesy against the shepherds of Israel; prophesy and say to them: 'This is what the Sovereign* LORD *says: Woe to you shepherds of Israel who only take care of yourselves! Should not shepherds take care of the flock?*
>
> [4] *You have not strengthened the weak or healed the sick or bound up the injured. You have not brought back the strays or searched for the lost. You have ruled them harshly and brutally.*

Brother Robison then quoted from parts of Jeremiah 23, which I have also quoted in a previous chapter and do again here.

Jeremiah 23:21-40:

> [21] *I did not send these prophets,*
> *yet they have run with their message;*
> *I did not speak to them,*
> *yet they have prophesied.*
> [22] *But if they had stood in my council,*
> *they would have proclaimed my words to my people*
> *and would have turned them from their evil ways*
> *and from their evil deeds.*

23 "Am I only a God nearby,"
declares the LORD,
"and not a God far away?
24 Who can hide in secret places
so that I cannot see them?"
declares the LORD.
"Do not I fill heaven and earth?"
declares the LORD.

25 "I have heard what the prophets say who prophesy lies
in my name. They say, 'I had a dream! I had a dream!'
26 How long will this continue in the hearts of these lying
prophets, who prophesy the delusions of their own minds?
27 They think the dreams they tell one another will make
my people forget my name, just as their ancestors forgot
my name through Baal worship. *28 Let the prophet who*
has a dream recount the dream, **but let the one who has**
my word speak it faithfully. For what has straw to do
with grain?" *declares the* LORD. *29* **"Is not my word**
like fire," *declares the* LORD, **"and like a hammer that**
breaks a rock in pieces?

30 "Therefore," declares the LORD, *"I am against the*
prophets who steal from one another words supposedly
from me. *31 Yes," declares the* LORD, *"I am against the*
prophets who wag their own tongues and yet declare, 'The
LORD *declares.'32 Indeed, I am against those who prophesy*
false dreams," declares the LORD. *"They tell them and*
lead my people astray with their reckless lies, yet I did not
send or appoint them. They do not benefit these people
in the least," declares the LORD.

He went on to talk about us not relying on the flesh "put no confidence
in the flesh (Phil. 3:3)" meaning not to rely on denominations, or
traditions, or preachers like himself and other leaders, but only lean on
the Word of God. He said:

"We are still looking to the flesh, not the Word. Listen, you couldn't tell a false prophet if you had one pastoring you every week. Because the only way you can know a false prophet is to know the truth and the truth is the Word of God."

I would add to that last sentence, the phrase "rightly divided." A little later James said:

"You better learn to refuse what I say. You better learn to refuse any man who is speaking, for the Word of God says to have no confidence in the flesh – any man's flesh." James later added: "You heap to yourselves teachers who will tickle your ears because you can't endure sound doctrine, and you are blown about by every wind and doctrine. You don't know what you believe. It doesn't matter what I say, it matters what He (God) says."

For clarity let me (not Brother Robison) quote what Ephesians 4:14 says completely:

14 Then we will no longer be infants, tossed back and forth by the waves, and blown here and there by every wind of teaching and by the cunning and craftiness of people in their deceitful scheming.

Brother James continued:

"We are just required to lean on the Word. Do you know where you are supposed to be when you leave here today? You are supposed to make a commitment to every word of God today, no matter what tradition says, no matter what Baptists say…"

Probably the most important thing James said in that sermon came almost at the end:

"Oh, I live for the day that we don't have followers of
W. A. Criswell and Adrian Rogers and James Robison,
we just have followers of Jesus."

I was in Texas at the time this happened and eight years before, had left the newly opened Criswell Center for Biblical Studies (named after the aforementioned W. A. Criswell) after having been there for only about a month in 1974. I left because the Dallas Baptist Association, led in part by the Chancellor of my Bible College, Dr. Criswell, came up with a policy that Charismatic Baptist churches had to desist operating in the gifts of the Holy Spirit or withdraw from the organization. Beverly Hills Baptist Church from Oak Cliff, Texas, near Dallas, was such a church, having healing prayer parts of services (as mentioned in James 5) and with some members operating in the gifts of tongues and the interpretation of tongues. Lulu Roman of "Hee Haw" fame got saved in that church around this time. They did not leave the organization or quit operating in the scriptural gifts of the Holy Spirit, so in 1975 the association kicked them out. Not satisfied with just disagreeing with Charismatics, Dr. Criswell went so far as to say in one speech to the Texas Baptist Convention in 1974, that speaking in tongues was "of the Devil." He likened it to the "babbling" that witches do. You can read about much of this is in the book, Bite Your Tongues, by Sandra Pratt Martin. Another Bible training school in the area, Dallas Theological Seminary, actually refused to accept students if they professed to speak in tongues. To be fair to the Baptists and others who disagree with those who believe in the Pentecostal gifts, I am including at the end of this chapter a discussion of the Bible texts they use as evidence for their position and some Bible texts and other reasons that show why I believe they have gotten it wrong.

James Robison was the bright shining star of all the evangelists in the Southern Baptist Convention and had much to lose if he fell out of favor with the denomination. So where was Brother Robison's loyalty when he made that speech I quoted from? Where was the loyalty of Pastor Howard Conatzer and other leaders of Beverly Hills Baptist Church when they bucked the denominational decree? Where was my loyalty when I dropped out of that Bible College due to the school founder's position and the leading of the Holy Spirit? Where is your loyalty today?

Our devotion and loyalty should always belong only to God and his holy Word. It should never be to a religious system, or a denomination or any organization, but only to God. That would be just having religion instead of relationship. We should never give in to a religious bully or group of them. W. A. Criswell once pastored the largest church (First Baptist of Dallas) in the largest protestant denomination in the country, which owned several whole blocks of downtown Dallas, making it probably the richest church in the denomination. Criswell was a past President of the Southern Baptist Convention. Billy Graham, who just changed addresses in recent years, was a member of his church at the time, so Dr. Criswell was the pastor of the man some called the nation's pastor. If there were such a thing as a Protestant Pope, he would have been it. I know I would have had much more traditional ministry success if I had stayed with the denominational route, but I have always tried to follow God, the Word, and my conscience, not a church or a pastor or anyone else. I would rather have Jesus "… than anything this world affords to give."

When you are in the right, that is, standing on the Word rightly divided (balanced), stand your ground and keep on doing what is right, regardless of what the "religious" people, or what your pastor, or what anyone else says. It is Christ you should be trying to please, not men. They may try to bully you and intimidate you into just keeping your mouth shut and "going along to get along," but you have a relationship with Christ and your strength comes from the Word of God, which is the Sword of the Spirit, and the Spirit of God. Remember that the Bible, the Sword of the Spirit (Eph. 6:17), is sharper than any two-edged sword (Heb. 4:12). It is what Jesus used to defeat Satan when He was being tempted by Lucifer who also quoted scripture and it is what Jesus used to correct many who opposed Him with unbalanced and incomplete views on scripture.

I want to include here a statement to make it clear that we run into unscriptural positions in probably all Christian organizations, denominations and non-denominational groups. It includes Protestants, Catholics, and Eastern Orthodox Christianity. My early background and that of James Robison was with Southern Baptists, but please see that this section deals with error of all kinds, from all sources. In fact, the people who I have nearly all my problems with regarding this fake faith, false prosperity teaching, are in the Pentecostal, full-gospel vein of denominations and groups, like I am.

Now, I want to discuss a little more how you handle the types of spiritual bullies I have described. Just like in setting boundaries with family members, coworkers, or friends, you have to know the standards of relationship you want to hold to and then require that if others want to maintain a relationship with you, then both you and they have to go by those standards. If they refuse to respect your standards, then you have to cut them off from relationship until they decide to accept and abide by your requirements. In business matters, you don't go into a contract that is not fair to you. In spiritual matters, we need to remember that the Bible is our first and only standard to go by. It outranks anyone else's opinion, regardless of how many degrees they have and how many positions they hold or have held. The Bible you read and study, as taught to you by the Holy Spirit, can eventually, once you become strong in knowledge of it, give you the confidence to stand your ground. In Jeremiah 15:19 God tells Jeremiah:

> [19] *Therefore this is what the* LORD *says:*
> *"If you repent, I will restore you*
> *that you may serve me;*
> *if you utter worthy, not worthless, words,*
> *you will be my spokesman.*
> *Let this people turn to you,*
> *but you must not turn to them.*

There are no more worthy words than scripture. If you study those words and gain a balance in them, you can stand. You need to take your stand and do not give in to spiritual bullies, but, let them come to you if they will. Some will and some will not. If they do not accept what you say and thus reject you, that is their loss, not yours. The only way you lose is if you give in to them. You are already fellowshipping with the best if you take your stand in Jesus.

As I will discuss more in the Appendix, once you have been studying the Bible for a while for yourself, not just reading the key verses your denomination or preacher teaches are important, you will be able to recognize when you hear something taught that does not line up with the Word and you will begin to go back and check out what they said, to see if it truly does or does not line up with the balance of scripture. If it does not, you can reject it and replace it. You can do what I call the "Three Rs" of discerning balanced doctrine. That is:

Recognize (error)
Reject it and
Replace it.

You replace it with what you believe is balanced doctrine. This is very empowering and a beginning in your becoming a strong believer.

In the next chapter I will address the sacred cow, the leaven of the Pharisees, that tradition of men taught as the commandment of God, called the tithe. In doing so, I will provide you with more Bible verses than most Christians ever thought existed about tithing to back up what I am teaching. You will be able to use these passages to instruct others and to defeat anyone who tries to oppose what you are saying. As you read, you might get angry and you might get perplexed at what you have and have not been taught, sometimes on purpose, sometimes out of ignorance, for however many years you have attended churches. With few exceptions, nearly all churches teach error on this topic and they are about to be exposed for either ignorance or greed or sometimes both, and in each case, false teaching.

Before I get to that however, as I said previously, I am including a discussion of what I was taught about the Pentecostal gifts when I was in non-Pentecostal churches. You may want to skip over this little section on Baptist and other non-Pentecostal Biblical interpretations if you already believe in the Pentecostal gifts. If so, you may want to come back to it later though, just to reinforce your beliefs.

SOME NON-PENTECOSTAL BIBLICAL INTERPRETATIONS AND TEACHINGS ON THE BAPTISM IN THE HOLY SPIRIT AND WHY THEY ARE WRONG

When I was attending Southern Baptist churches and when I was at Criswell Center for Biblical Studies in Dallas, which is now Criswell College, I was taught that we get all we are going to get of the Holy Spirit at salvation. I was also taught that although the gifts of the Holy Spirit, including tongues, did exist during the times of the Apostles, they died out after a couple of hundred years. They interpret part of a Bible verse from I Cor. 13 which I will quote later, that says, "when perfection comes," to mean when the cannon of the Bible was completed and we had the full 66 books of the Bible. In this case, they said the passage referred to the gifts of the Spirit like tongues no longer being needed after this perfection comes. As I said earlier in this chapter, I will try to show why I think these are very weak opinions and why I think they are very wrong.

First of all, regarding receiving the Holy Spirit at salvation, I fully agree with that, but not with that being the only time we can receive an impartation of him or empowering by him. Shortly after the crucifixion and resurrection of Jesus, but many days before the Day of Pentecost, the disciples, in John 20:21-22, were in a locked room for fear of the Jews and the resurrected Lord appeared to them saying:

> [21] Again Jesus said, "Peace be with you! As the Father has sent me, I am sending you." [22] And with that he breathed on them and said, "Receive the Holy Spirit.

These men had already believed in the resurrected Lord and he, through his breath gave them the Holy Spirit, so they were saved. Yet in Luke 24:49, also after his death, he tells them to tarry in Jerusalem until they are endued with power.

> [49] I am going to send you what my Father has promised; but stay in the city

We know this took place in Acts chapter two. Jesus also told them in the last chapter of Mark, in Mark 16:17-18:

> *[17] And these signs will accompany those who believe: In my name they will drive out demons; they will speak in new tongues; [18] they will pick up snakes with their hands; and when they drink deadly poison, it will not hurt them at all; they will place their hands on sick people, and they will get well."*

When Peter and the rest of the believers did receive that power through the Holy Spirit on the day of Pentecost, Acts 2:15-17 tells us Peter told the crowd this was what was spoken of by the prophet Joel. In verse 17, as Peter is quoting Joel, he says it was for the "last days." You can read the full quote which is Acts 2:15-21. Actually, Jesus quotes some of the same parts of Joel 2 that Peter quotes in Acts 2, when in Matthew 24, speaking of the time of His return to rapture the church (definitely last days stuff), He says in verse 29:

> *[29] "Immediately after the distress of those days*
> *"'the sun will be darkened,*
> *and the moon will not give its light;*
> *the stars will fall from the sky,*
> *and the heavenly bodies will be shaken.'*

Indeed, this is what Joel says <u>right after</u> he gets through saying "I will pour out my Spirit in those days, and they will prophesy." See Acts 2: 17-20; and Joel 2:28-31.

If the events of that day were in the last days, as Peter and Joel and Jesus said, how are we not in the last days, these nearly 2000 years later? Also, when Jesus said "these signs will accompany those who believe," He did not put a time limit on that anywhere. The Apostle Paul wrote in I Cor. 14:12 that some of the gifts build up the church, and since there are more people dying and going to hell now than ever before, how is it that some people think we don't need to build up the church now if we can? The Baptists I knew and others, seem to think that we are somehow in the Version 2.0 of the New Covenant, the one without the gifts of the Holy Spirit. If somebody sends you that "software," don't download it. I will show more about why I think they are wrong.

The passages I was taught most about the gifts of the Holy Spirit not being for today, come from I Cor. 13 and 14; and Eph. 4 and part of 5. I will start with I Cor. 13:8-12:

> 8 *Love never fails. But where there are prophecies, they will cease; where there are tongues, they will be stilled; where there is knowledge, it will pass away.* 9 *For we know in part and we prophesy in part,* 10 *but when completeness comes, what is in part disappears.* 11 *When I was a child, I talked like a child, I thought like a child, I reasoned like a child. When I became a man, I put the ways of childhood behind me.* 12 *For now we see only a reflection as in a mirror; then we shall see face to face. Now I know in part; then I shall know fully, even as I am fully known.*

This is the NIV version so in verse ten, where it says "completeness," the KJV says perfection. This is what I was taught meant when the Bible was completed and we had all 66 books. A problem with that interpretation is where he writes that when this perfection or completion comes, vs. 12, it says we will *"see face to face,"* also, *"then I shall know fully."* We do not see God face to face now nor will we know and understand things of God fully until the next life. When perfection comes it is when Jesus comes back to gather the redeemed. Then we truly will know and understand all spiritual truths fully, not before. When we are with the Lord, we will have no need for tongues or prophecy and they will be stilled.

They use the part about the childish things to say that compared to the Bible, these gifts are childish and the Bible is the mature and complete way of ministering to the Church. They may think then that Paul was an extremely childish person because in 14:18-19 of that book he says:

> [18] I thank God that I speak in tongues more than all
> of you. [19] But in the church I would rather speak five
> intelligible words to instruct others than ten thousand
> words in a tongue.

Here Paul is not saying that praying in a tongue is wrong, but that in the church meetings around other believers, it is much more profitable to only speak in a tongue if there is someone there to interpret the tongue. In that chapter he also talks about prophecy in the known language of the people hearing it, which is also profitable. He says in 14:39:

> [39] Therefore, my brothers and sisters, be eager to prophesy,
> and do not forbid speaking in tongues.

This forbidding to speak in tongues is exactly what the Texas Baptist Convention and the Dallas Baptist Association were doing in the 1970's. Evidently some people even in Paul's day were trying to stop the spiritual gifts from operating in services all together. Paul does talk about there needing to be good order in the services and I am ashamed to say that many Pentecostal churches do not go by these orderly guidelines and bring reproach on their denominations and non-denominational groups alike because of their lack of discipline. Some years ago a Pentecostal pastor, whom I challenged about this told me "Well, I would rather have a little wild fire than no fire at all." I left that church quickly because the pastor refused to follow the clear direction of scripture. I don't need that kind of fellowship. It is easy to see why some Baptists and other denominations tend to mock some of the things Pentecostals do, but the pride and arrogance many of the non-Pentecostals show in dealing with this issue, I think is worse behavior than the disorderly services of Pentecostals. Frankly, pride and arrogance are destructive to any kind of spiritual growth and maturity.

As I said, the passages some Baptists and other non-Pentecostals use, to say the gifts are not for today, are found mainly in I Corinthians 13 and 14. Let's back up a little and start in chapter 12, beginning in vs 4:

⁴ There are different kinds of gifts, but the same Spirit distributes them. ⁵ There are different kinds of service, but the same Lord. ⁶ There are different kinds of working, but in all of them and in everyone it is the same God at work.

⁷ Now to each one the manifestation of the Spirit is given for the common good. ⁸ To one there is given through the Spirit a message of wisdom, to another a message of knowledge by means of the same Spirit, ⁹ to another faith by the same Spirit, to another gifts of healing by that one Spirit, ¹⁰ to another miraculous powers, to another prophecy, to another distinguishing between spirits, to another speaking in different kinds of tongues,[a] and to still another the interpretation of tongues.[b] ¹¹ All these are the work of one and the same Spirit, and he distributes them to each one, just as he determines.

As Pentecostals know, and as these verses show, the gifts of the Holy Spirit consist of more than just tongues. Paul continues in verses 27-30:

²⁷ Now you are the body of Christ, and each one of you is a part of it. ²⁸ And God has placed in the church first of all apostles, second prophets, third teachers, then miracles, then gifts of healing, of helping, of guidance, and of different kinds of tongues. ²⁹ Are all apostles? Are all prophets? Are all teachers? Do all work miracles? ³⁰ Do all have gifts of healing? Do all speak in tongues[a]? Do all interpret?

Of course, Paul is asking these last several questions as rhetorical in nature and the answer is an understood "no." Paul discusses this same line of thought in Ephesians 4:11-13, where he says:

¹¹ So Christ himself gave some to be apostles, some to be prophets, some to be evangelists, and some to be pastors and teachers, to prepare God's people for works of service, so that the body of Christ may be built up until we all

> *reach unity in the faith and in the knowledge of the Son of God and become mature, attaining to the whole measure of the full-ness of Christ.*

This last quotation is referred to as the listing of the five-fold ministry. Most of these non-Pentecostal denominational groups, however, ignore the first two, the apostles and the prophets. By the time the non-Pentecostals get through removing the giftings they do not use and the ministry offices they do not allow, they are a three-fold ministry and they have less ways to build up the body of Christ than God intended *"for the common good."*

Paul talks about what signs mark an apostle in II Cor. 12:12:

> *The things that mark an apostle - signs, wonders and miracles - were done among you with great perseverance."*

So, if apostles perform signs and miracles and prophets get supernatural insight and words from God for people, and the Baptists and Presbyterians and others think those things are no longer happening, it is easy to see why you never see any of these in their churches. This reminds me of the types of people who were proud and headstrong, among other things, who Paul described in II Tim. 3:5 as *"having a form of godliness, but denying its power, from such turn away."*

In Southern Baptist circles I was told by some that prophecy can mean forth-tellers and not just foretellers. That was a way they used to explain away why there were no prophets in their churches. A major problem with that is that the five-fold ministry passage I quoted, already listed pastors and teachers and both of those are forth-tellers of the Word, so why would scripture need to list something different? They also said that apostles died out, like tongues and other miraculous signs, when we got the Bible. It would have been easy for the Holy Spirit to have inspired men to clearly write that time limitation into the Word of God if that was so but, the only time limitation mentioned is that it would happen in the last days. Guess where we are timewise today!

Clearly it is most important that a person gets saved. Getting saved always comes first and then, for some, the Baptism in the Holy Spirit, as

I will show in scripture. I would rather attend a Baptist church that only taught about salvation and never about the Baptism in the Holy Spirit, than I would a Pentecostal church that never taught about salvation and only about the gifts of the Spirit. Actually, I left a Full-Gospel church (which is a type of Pentecostal church) for that very reason. The greatest miracle that anyone can receive today is salvation! So, if you do not believe in miracles happening today, then you do not believe in salvation happening today either. When you receive the quickening of the Holy Spirit at salvation, you are receiving life. When you receive the Baptism in the Holy Spirit, you are receiving power for service to God. Actually, when I received it, there were not any people around me who fully understood what had happened (including me). I knew I had received some kind of power from God when this happened. I had heard about tongues and read about them in the Bible, but only one person I knew had ever prayed in tongues. He was a retired Green Beret who became a pastor and had been asked to leave his Baptist church after he shared about speaking in tongues. He did not know much about it either, but wrote down some of what he heard himself say and asked a college religious studies professor about it later. She told him it was ancient Hebrew, which he had never studied.

I have heard taught and believe it is true, that there are pictures or types of these two baptisms (the one in water and the one in the Holy Spirit) in the Old Testament from when the Jews came out of Egypt. Egypt was symbolic of sin and after the first Passover (which symbolized salvation), when the Jewish people passed through the Red Sea, that was the biggest of these two symbolic baptisms, baptism by water. They came out of sin and into a life of following God and being guided by him. They left those old ways behind. The second symbolic baptism, that of the baptism in the Holy Spirit, was when they finally crossed the Jordan and went into the "promised land." Even though the Jordan was nowhere near as big as the Red Sea, it still took a miraculous occurrence to get them across (see Joshua 3).

Some gospel songs portray going to heaven as "crossing over Jordan" but, there will not be any fighting or struggling in heaven as there was when the Jews went into Canaan. I think crossing the Jordan is more about moving into what God wants us to be, to have, and to do.

The Jordan River however, did serve as a natural boundary against the enemies of the Jewish tribes that did cross over and stayed. But not all Jews crossed over to take possession of land in Canaan where God originally purposed. Two and a half tribes stayed on the Gilead side of the Jordan and took their inheritance there after asking permission to do that. The men did cross over to help their brothers with the fighting, but then returned to their families in Gilead. They never really got what God had envisioned for them, and even though what they did receive seemed pretty good to them, I believe they would have been better off on the promised land side of the river. You do not have to receive the Baptism in the Holy Spirit to be saved, just like they were still in the Jewish faith even though they did not possess Canaan themselves. However, in Gilead they were more easily swayed into turning away from their true faith, both from within and from the nations around them, than the Jews on the other side were; and when those pagan nations decided to attack them, they were more vulnerable than those on the Canaan side. Part of the reason we benefit so much from the Baptism in the Holy Spirit is because it helps us in our spiritual warfare against the enemy. I think the analogy is clear.

For some people in the Bible, the Holy Spirit Baptism was given right after they got saved, like Cornelius' family and household, as stated in Acts: 10:22-48 and 11:15-17. For others, there seems to have been a delay between believing in Christ and receiving this experience, as stated in Acts 19:1-7. In any case, I do not believe God gives this Baptism to people who do not want it. I believe he works within our free-will. Scripture does say in Luke 11:13 that God will give the Holy Spirit to people who want it, though he could be talking about the salvation quickening dose or the Holy Spirit Baptism empowering dose, or both:

> [13] *If you then, though you are evil, know how to give good gifts to your children, how much more will your Father in heaven give the Holy Spirit to those who ask him!"*

One passage that seems to explain part of why we need this Baptism is about how it helps us to pray effectively. Rom. 8:26-27 says:

26 Likewise the Spirit also helps in our weaknesses. For we do not know what we should pray for as we ought, but the Spirit Himself makes intercession for us with groanings which cannot be uttered. 27 Now He who searches the hearts knows what the mind of the Spirit is, because He makes intercession for the saints according to the will of God.

One more argument some non-Pentecostals have used in the past to explain away scriptures about speaking in tongues is that this is just where God taught them how to speak in a foreign language. Please read any passage where people received these tongues which were associated with the Baptism in the Holy Spirit, like Acts 2, and tell me that you honestly think the context and words make you believe someone just learned that language. Berlitz is the oldest company I know of that teaches languages to people, though there are many more such companies now. None of these can teach anyone a language within a period of a few seconds. Paul even says when a person prays in an unknown tongue, his mind does not understand it. See I Cor. 14:14-15:

14 For if I pray in a tongue, my spirit prays, but my mind is unfruitful. 15 So what shall I do? I will pray with my spirit, but I will also pray with my understanding; I will sing with my spirit, but I will also sing with my understanding.

Of course, if we learn a foreign language, we learn the meanings of each word and/or phrase.

NOT A FELLOWSHIP BREAKER

Now, a believer does not have to believe the same as I do on disputable matters for me to have fellowship with him/her in Christ. If someone has accepted Jesus as their savior, they are my brother or sister in Christ and I will do what I can to be in fellowship with them. If someone does not believe in the Holy Spirit Baptism and in the gifts of the Holy Spirit being still for today, we can agree to disagree on those things. I do not have to change my beliefs and he/she will not change their mind by my being dogmatic and getting all upset with them. If they do change their mind it will be because I gently shared with them what I believe and why, and then left it to them and to the Holy Spirit working within them, to do the convincing. He might even give them this baptism and then they will believe in it for sure.

Nobody should believe what I say because I said it, but only because they also studied scripture and came to that conclusion themselves or because they experienced it themselves and then understood it from scripture. Paul said about the Berean church that they were more honorable than those in Thessalonica because they searched the scriptures daily to see if what he said was true (Acts 17:11). I believe that no church should throw people out of their fellowship because they believe scripture a little differently than they do, as long as it is on disputable matters. Salvation is the key to get you into the family of God. That should be the main key to fellowship within our spiritual family. Being patient in dealing with and in instructing others who may be wrong in some of their beliefs, will keep you from being a spiritual bully and help people in the world and in the church to be drawn to your message and our Jesus.

Lastly, just like there are false prophets, apostles and teachers, there are fakers when it comes to the spiritual gifts. There are fake faith healers and even fake tongues. I have heard some fake tongues and seen fake faith healers. That certainly does not mean all who exercise the gifts are fakes. I believe the fakes are only a small minority. That is one reason there is a gift of discernment given to some in the Church. We certainly need that to help keep us on the right path.

MY PERSONAL EXPERIENCE:

I had been saved for twelve years before this experience happened to me but, I had been in fervent prayer for about a month before this, asking God to help me in several areas of my life. I was fresh out of the Marines and one of the things I was praying for was some emotional healing over things that had happened in my life both before and during my hitch in the Marines. I felt kind of dead inside and was hoping for a return of some type of joy in my life. I also had a smoking habit I could not break and a bad respiratory tract infection, probably bronchitis. So, I was also praying for God to help me quit smoking, both to end the nasty cigarette habit and to help get rid of that illness.

When "it" happened, in addition to giving me the Baptism in the Holy Spirit, God also healed me of the bronchitis and totally delivered me from nicotine addiction, all at the same time. Nobody even touched me; no preacher ever laid hands on me. I felt like going down to the altar at the end of an evening service to pray and the moment my knees hit the carpet, things began to happen. I don't know anyone else who got healed and delivered from cigarettes when they received the Baptism in the Holy Spirit, I just know I did. I guess God was working on this messed up vessel for about five minutes or so, cleaning and healing, and filling. When the work was through and I began to calm down a little, I had a joy I could not explain and felt like I was walking a couple of inches off the ground for several days. There was a power in me and a sensitivity to the Holy Spirit I had never known before. The Bible became clearer and more meaningful than it had ever been. I did not even want a cigarette after that and have not had one for 47 years. The congestion in my chest that had been so bad, was about 95% gone and cleared up completely in a few days. So, my own experience tells me the non-Pentecostals who believe this experience is not for today, are wrong.

When I prayed about why God had given me this experience, this power, and about how I was supposed to use it, the words I got back from God, in my spirit, were that it was "For the work of the ministry." Truly, all of the gifts of the Holy Spirit are to be used for edifying the Body of Christ, to include oneself. As I said, that was about 47 years ago and God has been faithful and helped me to minister some, but no believer is through ministering until they draw that last breath. The Holy Spirit within us continues to motivate us to serve God and helps us to do so. I hope some of my more effective days are still before me.

CHAPTER 8

TRUTH AND LIES ABOUT TITHING – INCLUDING THE SCRIPTURE PASSAGES MOST PASTORS WON'T TEACH

Revolutionary is not too bold a word to describe the message I have found in studying tithing. The first thing I found was that two main activities seem to be involved in tithing, besides providing for pastors and the church buildings, as important as I believe those things are. I also discovered that the traditional teaching about tithing in churches today, was and is inaccurate in a number of ways. To begin with, even if all New Covenant believers were still under the Mosaic law, and we are not, what is currently taught about tithing would not even be close to accurate for us today and since we are not under the law, we need to make decisions about how the principles behind the Mosaic tithe requirement may actually apply to us today, and we need to look at anything else the Bible teaches us about the importance of giving.

I found that the traditional teaching on tithing today leaves out the two main activities involved in Old Testament tithing other than the provision for ministers and buildings. These are: (1) Spending time with God in order to become strong in our faith and to be able to be the ministers to those around us that we should be; (2) Providing for the poor (widows, orphans, and otherwise destitute) so they could spend time with God also. A third point this study will clearly show is that the common teaching today on the tithe, that is, the legalistic requirement of all Christians to bring a tenth of their income to the church, is not supported by the **balance** of both New and Old Testament scripture! In the following pages, we will look at all scripture on this subject, not just ones used by the tithe promoters, and let the reader make up his or her own mind. I will present the verses that if taken by themselves would promote the commonly taught version of this doctrine, but unlike other preachers and teachers, I will also show readers what I guess the late Paul Harvey would have called "the rest of the story."

It is not the purpose of this chapter of the book to encourage greediness or in any way to discourage giving. It is simply to be truthful, to remove bondage from the backs of some believers, and to set the record straight. I will do this by first explaining how tithing was supposed to work in the Mosaic Covenant and what the New Covenant teaches about it. Next, I will discuss the importance of spending time with God and show the necessity for the believer to be helping the less fortunate among us. I will begin by stating what most people know about tithing.

Malachi 3:7-12 (NIV) says:

> *"Ever since the time of your forefathers you have turned away from my decrees and have not kept them. Return to me, and I will return to you," says the Lord Almighty. "But you ask, 'How are we to return?' Will a man rob God? Yet you rob me." "But you ask, 'How do we rob you?'" "In tithes and offerings.*
>
> *You are under a curse--the whole nation of you--because you are robbing me. Bring the whole tithe into the storehouse, that there may be food in my house. Test me in this," says the Lord Almighty, "and see if I will not throw open the floodgates of heaven and pour out so much blessing that you will not have room enough for it.*

I will prevent pests from devouring your crops, and the vines in your fields will not cast their fruit," says the Lord Almighty. "Then all the nations will call you blessed, for yours will be a delightful land," says the Lord Almighty."

I quote this because it is the most commonly used passage I have heard concerning tithing. Unfortunately, it is often taught as if it is the only passage in the Bible on tithing or how tithing worked. In truth, you have to really read a lot more of the Bible to understand how Malachi three actually fits in with the rest of the Bible on this topic. This passage just scratches the surface, so to speak.

It is obvious in the above passage that God is addressing people who knew the Old Testament tithe laws and who had not been keeping them. The problem is that most Christians today do not know the Mosaic Covenant tithe laws or the principles found in them. The next group of scripture passages I would like to comment on are rather lengthy but it is important to read them all because they outline the Mosaic law's requirements concerning tithing and bring out how the tithe law in chapter 14 of Dt. is interrelated with the laws regarding the sabbatical year, jubilee year, and the laws concerning feasts, found in the next two chapters of that book. I am underlining some passages for emphasis. They begin with: Dt. 14:22-29:

> *Be sure to set aside a tenth of all that your fields produce each year. **Eat** the tithe of your grain, new wine and oil, and the firstborn of your herds and flocks in the presence of the Lord your God at the place he will choose as a dwelling for his Name, so that you may learn to revere the Lord your God always. But if that place is too distant and you have been blessed by the Lord your God and cannot carry your tithe (because the place where the Lord will choose to put his Name is too far away), then exchange your tithe for silver, and take the silver with you and go to the place the Lord your God will choose. Use the silver to buy whatever you like: cattle, sheep, wine or other fermented drink, or anything you wish. Then you*

and your household shall eat there in the presence of the Lord your God and rejoice. And do not neglect the Levites living in your towns, for they have no allotment or inheritance of their own.

*At the end of **every three years**, bring all the tithes of that year's produce and store it in your towns, so that the Levites (who have no allotment or inheritance of their own) and the aliens, the fatherless and the widows who live in your towns may come and eat and be satisfied, and so that the Lord your God may bless you in all the work of your hands.*

Notice please that from Dt. 14, we see there are two different methods for using the tithes; one for the "each year" tithe and another for the "every third year" tithe. We will see more on this as we go.

The next passage is lengthy, but outlines the three times a year Jewish men had to travel to the tabernacle and later, to the temple in Jerusalem for worship and the length of those stays. This is important because these were the times and events involved with the using by the Jewish people of the yearly tithe and the offerings of other things required by the law of Moses. Please read Dt. 15:19-16:17:

Set apart for the Lord your God every firstborn male of your herds and flocks. Do not put the firstborn of your oxen to work, and do not shear the firstborn of your sheep. Each year you and your family are to eat them in the presence of the Lord your God at the place he will choose. If an animal has a defect, is lame or blind, or has any serious flaw, you must not sacrifice it to the Lord your God. You are to eat it in your own towns. Both the ceremonially unclean and the clean may eat it, as if it were gazelle or deer. But you must not eat the blood; pour it out on the ground like water.

Observe the month of Abib and celebrate the Passover of the Lord your God, because in the month of Abib he brought you out of Egypt by night. Sacrifice as the Passover to the Lord your God an animal from your flock or herd at the place the Lord will choose as a dwelling for his Name. Do not eat it with the bread made with yeast, but for seven days eat unleavened bread, the bread of affliction, because you left Egypt in haste--so that all the days of your life you may remember the time of your departure from Egypt. Let no yeast be found in your possession in all your land for seven days. Do not let any of the meat you sacrifice on the evening of the first day remain until morning.

You must not sacrifice the Passover in any town the Lord your God gives you except in the place he will choose as a dwelling for his Name. There you must sacrifice the Passover in the evening, when the sun goes down, on the anniversary of your departure from Egypt. Roast it and eat it at the place the Lord your God will choose. Then in the morning return to your tents. For six days eat unleavened bread and on the seventh day hold an assembly to the Lord your God and do not work.

Count off seven weeks from the time you begin to put the sickle to the standing grain. Then celebrate the Feast of Weeks to the Lord your God by giving a freewill offering in proportion the blessings the Lord your God has given you. And rejoice before the Lord your God at the place he will choose as a dwelling for his Name--you, your sons and daughters, your menservants and maidservants, the Levites in your towns, and the aliens, the fatherless and the widows living among you. Remember that you were slaves in Egypt, and follow carefully these decrees. Celebrate the Feast of Tabernacles for seven days after you have gathered the produce of your threshing floor and your winepress. Be joyful at your Feast--you, your sons and daughters, your menservants and maidservants, and the Levites, the aliens, fatherless and the widows who live in your towns. For seven days celebrate the Feast to the Lord your God at the place the Lord will choose. For the Lord your God will bless you in all the work of your hands, and your joy will be complete.

<u>Three times a year all your men must appear before the Lord your God at the place he will choose: at the Feast of Unleavened Bread, the Feast of Weeks and the Feast of Tabernacles.</u> No man should appear before the Lord empty-handed: Each of you must bring a gift in proportion to the way the Lord your God has blessed you.

Next, we see another passage dealing with the third-year tithe and how it was to be used. Dt. 26:12-15 rephrases 14:28-29:

<u>When you have finished setting aside a tenth of all your produce in the third year, the year of the tithe, you shall give it to the Levite, the alien, the fatherless and the widow, so that they may eat in your towns and be satisfied. Then say to the Lord your God</u>: "I have removed from my house the sacred portion and have given it to the Levite, the alien, the fatherless and the widow, according to all you commanded. I have not turned aside from your commands nor have I forgotten any of them. I have not eaten any of the sacred portion while I was in mourning, nor have I removed any of it while I was unclean, nor have I offered any of it to the dead. I have obeyed the Lord my God; I have done everything you commanded me. Look down from heaven, your holy dwelling place, and bless your people Israel and the land you have given us as you promised on oath to our forefathers, a land flowing with milk and honey."

Next, we see what portion of the third-year tithe (the Levite's tithe) went to the temple. Here it is called "the Lord's portion." Please read Num. 18:26-29:

> "*Speak to the Levites and say to them: 'When you receive from the Israelites the tithe I give you as your inheritance, you must present a tenth of that tithe as the Lord's offering.* Your offering will be reckoned to you as grain from the threshing floor or juice from the winepress. *In this way you also will present an offering to the Lord from all the tithes you receive from the Israelites. From these tithes you must give the Lord's portion to Aaron the priest. You must present as the Lord's portion the best and holiest part of everything given to you.*

Neh. 10:38 restates a portion of the above passage regarding the part of the tithe that was to be taken to the storehouse which Mal. 3 refers to.

> A *priest descended from Aaron is to accompany the Levites when they receive the tithes, and the Levites are to bring a tenth of the tithes* up to the house of our God, to the storerooms of the treasury.

Nehemiah was written less than the average person's lifetime before the book of Malachi was written, so when I conclude that it was this one tenth of the Levite's tithe (the every third year tithe you have been reading about), that was referred to by Malachi in chapter 3 of that book, it is with very good reason,

After reading Dt. 16:1-17, it is obvious that the three times a year of coming to the tabernacle, or later, the temple, and traveling all that way with enough food, not just for you and your family, but also bringing enough for the Levites, widows, fatherless, etc., to spend a week of eating and worshipping and hearing the scripture taught, and this being in conjunction with the different harvest times of the different crops (as the feast days were), is the method and time for the giving of the tithe, at least for the first two years out of three. To be specific, this regular yearly tithe was clearly to be set aside for consumption by the people themselves during these three times of worship. The third-year tithe was probably an extra amount to be set aside because God still wanted the Israelites to come to Jerusalem to worship during those three times a year. Leviticus chapter 23 goes into a lot more detail about the various feast days and if you have not studied those, you may want to read that later.

In Leviticus 25:1-12, we see the laws concerning the sabbatical year and part of the laws regarding the jubilee year:

> The Lord said to Moses on Mount Sinai, "Speak to the Israelites and say to them: 'When you enter the land I am going to give you, the land itself must observe a Sabbath to the Lord. For six years sow your fields, and for six years prune your vineyards and gather their crops. But in the seventh year the land is to have a Sabbath of rest, a Sabbath to the Lord. Do not sow your fields or prune your vineyards. Do not reap what grows of itself or harvest the grapes of your untended vines. The land is to have a year of rest. Whatever the land yields during the Sabbath year will be food for you--for yourself, your manservant and maidservant, and the hired worker and temporary resident who live among you, as well as for your livestock and the wild animals in your land. Whatever the land produces may be eaten. Count off seven Sabbaths of years--seven times seven years--so that the seven Sabbaths of years amount to a period of forty-nine years. Then have the trumpet sounded everywhere on the tenth day of the seventh month; on the Day of Atonement sound the trumpet throughout your land. Consecrate the fiftieth year and proclaim liberty throughout the land to all its inhabitants. It shall be a jubilee for you; each one of you is to return to his family property and each to his own clan. The fiftieth year shall be a jubilee for you; do not sow and do not reap what grows of itself or harvest the untended vines. For it is a jubilee and is to be holy for you; eat only what is taken directly from the fields.

Chapter 15 of Deuteronomy discusses Jubilee years also, if you would like to look at it. These verses fit in with the third-year tithe being special for the Levites and priests because the sixth year, which was a second third year in a seven-year cycle, was a higher produce year, preceding a year of no crops (see quote following). By giving a tithe to the Levites and priests on that double (or some say triple) produce year, the recipients would have enough to make it through the lean provisions coming up. Leviticus 25:20-22 states:

> You may ask, "What will we eat in the seventh year if we do not plant or harvest our crops?" I will send you such a blessing in the sixth year that the land will yield enough for three years. While you plant during the eighth year, you will eat from the old crop and will continue to eat from it until the harvest of the ninth year comes in.

Because it was enough for three years, it seems that it would also cover the two year period without crops during a sabbath year before the Jubilee year, and then the Jubilee year itself.

The following table shows an overview of how the sabbatical and Jubilee year system worked:

A SEVEN YEAR CYCLE OF MOSAIC COVENANT TITHING

First year	The Israelite man set aside a tenth of his crops and other income and used it to provide for himself, any of his family that wanted to come, and the poor and fatherless in the area that wanted to come, to be able to have food to eat while traveling to and from the Tabernacle/Temple three times a year, to also be able to eat while they spent a week or eight days, there in that place worshiping the Lord and hearing his Word read and taught by the priests during the feasts/festivals of the Lord.
Second year	Same as the first.

Third year	This was where, probably in addition to the regular tithe for the Jews, they gave the Levites a tithe that was used for the widows, the orphans, the poor, and the Levites living in that area who would come from their towns to the towns of the other Israelites and collect that tithe and keep 90% of it for themselves as part of their pay for the work of the Tabernacle/Temple, and give the other tenth to the Priests who worked at the Temple as part of their pay. The priests also got portions of all the offerings they killed and offered for the Israelites as the rest of their pay.
Fourth year	Same as the first-year events listed above.
Fifth year	Same as the first-year events.
Sixth year	God gave a double or triple crop (see Lev. 25:20-22) so everyone mentioned in the third year above would be taken care of during the sabbatical (seventh) year which followed because there was to be no planting of crops in the seventh year. This was a second, third year, which meant it had the extra tithe meant for Levites. It was enough for them to cover them during the no planting period. Everyone was provided for, the poor, the regular Israelite, the Levite, and the priests.
Seventh year	There were to be no crops, but the normal worship continued three times a year because of the increased crop the year before. The next seven- year cycle would start after this one was completed. After seven of these seven-year cycles, there would be a Jubilee year with no crops but, as stated already, Lev. 25: 20-22 said the sixth year before that last sabbatical year would produce "enough" to last for three years.

See how Neh. 10:38 fits with Dt. 14:28-29 and the familiar Mal. 3:10. As stated, Nehemiah was written only about 55 years or less before Malachi; see how Neh. 12:44 and 47 describe the reestablishment of this system after the return from Babylonian captivity:

> *At that time men were appointed to be in charge of the*
> *storerooms for the contributions, first-fruits and tithes.*
> *From the fields around the towns they were to bring into*
> *the storerooms (in the towns) the portions required by the*
> *Law for the priests and the Levites, for Judah was pleased*
> *with the ministering priests and Levites. (47) They also*
> *set aside the portion for the other Levites, and the Levites*
> *set aside the portion for the descendants of Aaron (the*
> *family the priests came from).*

This last portion (vs. 47) was the portion that went to the temple storerooms or storehouse. If the whole tithe of the entire nation of Israel had been brought into the storehouse of the temple each year, (as is taught by most preachers), there would have been: (1) no provision for the people to travel and to spend 3 weeks a year worshipping and eating the tithe in the presence of their God as scripture required; (2) no provision for the poor and fatherless to eat out of the tithe as scripture required; (3) no provision for the Levites living in the various Levitical cities located around the countryside; (4) nowhere near enough room to put it all, even in Malachi's day there were way too many people; the whole temple would not have held the tithe, let alone the storehouse; (5) way too much for the priests and the others designated to eat from the storehouse to eat.

The part of the total tithe of grain that came to the storehouse in the Temple was, as you have read, a tenth of the Levite's tithe, which was given every third year. It is less clear if this is an additional tithe on a third year or if it is just a different use of the tithe for that year. Another interpretation that would be compatible with all of scripture is that when Malachi said, *"Bring ye all the tithe into the storehouse, that there may be bread in my house,"* he was referring to the storehouse in the towns from which the Levites took their tithe every third year and then brought a tenth of it to the priests. Either interpretation works.

Malachi wrote his words about 55 years, or possibly less (depending on the commentary), after Neh. 10, 11 and 13 were written and it is obvious that the tithe law was not being carried out. We know that the Jews did not keep the Sabbath year requirement to not plant crops because this is mentioned as one of the reasons for the length of the Babylonian captivity (2 Chron. 36:21). They also did not keep the feasts as they should, which we know because of Hezekiah's and Josiah's reforms, (2 Chron. 35:18), and from Nehemiah's reforms, (Neh. 8:17). From Mal. Chapter 3, we know that they were not giving tithes soon after the captivity ended. It seems that most of Israel was falling short on all aspects of the tithe, therefore, affecting the tithe that went to the storehouse. We also know that the people had misused the storehouse in the temple (Neh. 13:4-9):

> "Before this, Eliashib the priest had been put in charge of the storerooms of the house of our God. He was closely associated with Tobiah (a foreigner), and he had provided him with a large room formerly used to store the grain offerings and incense and temple articles, and also the tithes of grain, new wine and oil prescribed for the Levites, singers and gatekeepers, as well as the contributions for the priests.
>
> But while all this was going on, I was not in Jerusalem, for in the thirty-second year of Artaxerxes king of Babylon I had returned to the king. Some time later I asked his permission and came back to Jerusalem. Here I learned about the evil thing Eliashib had done in providing Tobiah a room in the courts of the house of God. I was greatly displeased and threw all Tobiah's household goods out of the room. I gave orders to purify the rooms, and then I put back into them the equipment of the house of God, with the grain offerings and the incense."

With a knowledge of all of these scriptures concerning the tithe laws and the tithe practices just prior to the writing of the Malachi passage most preachers use, it is only logical to conclude that it is this failure to follow the overall tithe laws, which then decreased the amount that went into the storehouse on the third year (that one tenth of the Levite's tithe, called the Lord's portion), that is obviously referred to in Malachi three.

There were other contributions beyond the tithe, which both Moses and Nehemiah required, which were probably not being met either, and which added to the frustration of Malachi. This described summary of how tithing was supposed to have worked is the only conclusion that fits with all of the scripture concerning tithing. If this is not yet clear to you, it would help to go back and read the chapter to this point again. I know it was a lot of scripture and probably difficult to totally absorb.

So, because the third-year tithe was given twice every seven years (the third and the sixth year) it was given 14 years out of 50, not every year. That is, only 28% of the years had a tithe other than what the Jewish people used for themselves, the poor, and the local Levites to eat.

After the return of the Jews from captivity (which included the time Malachi was written), these laws had not been removed from scripture nor had the Mosaic law gone out of effect. The territory the Jews lived in at that time, however, was smaller than it had been before captivity and it is possible there was a different method used for distributing the third-year tithe between the regular Levites and the actual priests. However, in any case, Nehemiah and Malachi were not teaching a different law, thus replacing what Moses had given them to follow, so the principles were the same.

We have been looking at the verses in the following tables, but these organize them for the reader.

Scriptures about the tithe laws:

Deuteronomy:	Dt.12:17-19; Dt.14:22-29; Dt.15:16 through chapt.16 vs.17; also Dt. 26:12-15
Numbers	Nm. 18:26-29
Nehemiah	Note: Both Nehemiah and Malachi were written after the return from captivity. Neh. 10:38; 12: 44, 47; These last two verses agree with Malachi 3:10. Nehemiah chapters 10, 11, and 12 show there were problems with the Jews giving the tithe and were written only about 55 years before Malachi.
Malachi	3:7-12

Scriptures about the Festivals/Feasts of the Lord:

Leviticus	All of chapter 23; chapter 25:20-22;

Scriptures about the sabbatical and Jubilee years

Leviticus	25:1-12

The arrival of a position on any point of doctrine that throws out 90% or more of the scripture on that doctrine, is a very poor one at best. The commonly preached interpretation of tithing, that is, taking Malachi three by itself, is not only a poor doctrinal position but, is rather suspect in motive.

SPENDING TIME WITH GOD

As I stated at the beginning of this chapter, the first activity I think tithing scriptures specifically emphasize is spending time with God. People were to leave their towns and villages and travel to the dwelling of God, many miles away. There were no churches in the towns (synagogues were not created until the Babylonian captivity of the Jews). This was their time to spend in God's presence. It appears that God intended for this time to be spent at His dwelling so that the priests could read the Word of God to the people and explain the meanings of it to them. This would help make them the people God wanted them to be. The best example found in scripture of this happening is in Neh. chapter eight. In verse 17 of that chapter it says in part that, "*their joy was very great,*" just as Dt. 14:26 had said it should be when it told them to eat in the presence of "*your God and rejoice.*" To the modern believer there is a direct parallel. Our joy and peace is greatly enhanced by spending time in prayer and Bible study and in church attendance (fellowship with God and with the saints).

In addition to the plain statements in scripture about spending time with God, there is something quite subtle that I believe shows this principle. Please bear with me for the next three paragraphs while I try to explain my theory about how spending time with God (tithing your time) ties into the 144,000 number mentioned in Revelation, because a tenth of our time a day is two hours and twenty four minutes, or 144 minutes. It is just a theory, but interesting.

Eph. 2:20-22 tells us, we are a building being placed upon the foundation of the apostles and prophets. Compare this with Revelation 21:12-14 which says that this city is built on gates named for the 12 patriarchs and foundations named for the 12 apostles. This is similar to the description of the Israel of God by Paul in Gal. 6:15-16, Rom. 9:6-8, and again, Eph. 2:20-22. The measurements of this city are also in 12's, more precisely, 12 x 12's.

Twelve times twelve is 144, (the measurement of the depth of the wall). It is interesting that chapter 7 of Rev. describes 144,000 that will be saved in verses 4-8 and then starting in verse 9, talks about a great multitude that no one could count, but it seems as though he is speaking of the same group. Please bear with me a little longer, I'm coming to my point. I believe that this 144,000 and the same number in chapter 14, is figurative only. I believe that it is simply a large multiple (1000), times the Old Testament saints (represented by the 12 patriarchs), times the New Testament saints (represented by the 12 apostles). If this 144,000 is symbolic of the overcoming church, sparkling like a gem stone, as I believe it is, then the number 144 is symbolic. As I said, a tenth (or tithe) of our time is 144 minutes a day. Think about that when you set aside time for God.

When the Jews spent 3 weeks a year, plus travel time to and from the feast site, it involved about a tenth of their time. Remember the trip Mary and Joseph took for Passover in Luke chapter two. Perhaps then, this speaks to us that by giving God a tithe of time, we will be helping ourselves to become that overcoming church, that New Jerusalem. Pray about it!

PROVIDING FOR THE POOR

The second emphasized activity in tithing other than providing for ministers and buildings, is provision for the poor. It is plain in Dt. 14 that the poor are to be provided for by the tithe, as well as the Levites and priests. What we did not look at in this chapter, though we did earlier in the book, are the curses that fell on Israel and other groups for failing to care for the poor. Ezekiel 16:49-50, tells us that one of the main reasons Sodom was judged was because it refused to help the poor, (not only for sexual sins), and it says that the Jews were living worse than Sodom.

Proverbs 28:27 says:

> *Those who give to the poor will lack nothing, but those who close their eyes to them receive many curses.*

I have heard a number of preachers talk about a curse for not giving the whole tithe to the church, but, I have only heard one speak of these curses for not helping the poor. Amos 2:5-7, 4:1-2; Dan. 4:27 and Dt. 15:7-11 are also good passages on the subject of providing for the poor: Deuteronomy 15:7-11 reads as follows:

> *"If there is a poor man among your brothers in any of the towns of the land that the Lord your God is giving you, do not be hardhearted or tightfisted toward your poor brother. Rather be openhanded and freely lend him whatever he needs. Be careful not to harbor this wicked thought: 'The seventh year, the year for canceling debts, is near,' so that you do not show ill will toward your needy brother and give him nothing. He may then appeal to the Lord against you, and you will be found guilty of sin. Give generously to him and do so without a grudging heart; then because of this the Lord your God will bless you in all your work and in everything you put your hand to. There will always be poor people in the land. Therefore, I command you to be openhanded toward your brothers and toward the poor and needy in your land."*

Notice the positive promise for helping the poor in Dt. 15; this is found often elsewhere in scripture. A concordance and an hour or so of page turning will reward you with plenty more evidence to prove the value of helping those less fortunate. Also, of interest is that, as I discussed earlier in the book, the main discussions of giving in the New Testament, have to do with collections for the poor, rather than giving to church activities of other nature. The books of Romans, I Corinthians, II Corinthians, and Galatians contain examples of this. Besides all the passages in II Corinthians 8 and 9 and other passages discussed in Chapter 4, we see the following:

Rom. 15:26:

> *"For Macedonia and Achaia were pleased to make a contribution for the poor among the saints in Jerusalem."*

In Gal. 2:10, speaking of his meeting with the church fathers in Jerusalem, Paul wrote:

> *"All they asked was that we should continue to remember the poor, the very thing I was eager to do."*

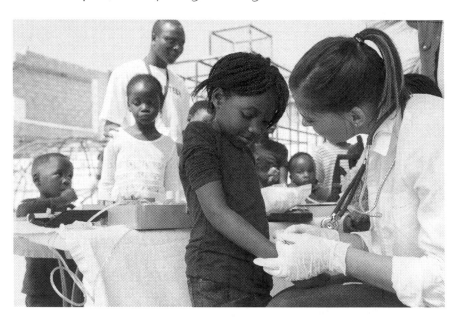

One mention of tithing to the Jewish Pharisee hypocrites before Jesus was crucified, thus while the law was still in effect, seems to be a warning against missing the most important point and part of the act of tithing; Lk. 11:42;

"Woe to you Pharisees, because you give God a tenth of your mint, rue and all other kinds of garden herbs, but you neglect justice and the love of God. You should have practiced the latter without leaving the former undone."

As stated already, I John 3:17 tells us that giving to the poor is practicing the love of God.

Earlier in the study, we saw that the common teaching today on tithing is not accurate even if you think we are still under the law. But, since we are no longer under the law, should we teach even a balanced version of Old Testament tithing as a requirement in the New Covenant? As stated, the passage above from Luke was written before the New Covenant began. That is, before the death, burial, and resurrection of Christ. It is significant enough to note that after Christ died and was resurrected, ushering in the New Covenant, the one and only reference to tithing in the rest of the New Testament, (that is after the New Covenant began) is an historical reference to Melchizedek and to the loftiness of his priesthood because Abraham gave a one-time tithe to him before the Law was given to Moses (see Heb. 7).

Furthermore, rejecting the burden of the law, the only requirements that the church fathers in Jerusalem gave to Paul for the gentile converts to Christianity were that they abstain from sexual immorality, abstain from meat offered to idols, the meat of strangled animals and blood, and to remember the poor (see Acts 15:21 and Gal. 2).

Some modern theology, as I have discussed in previous chapters, has excused the church from helping the poor to a great degree by saying that, "If they tithed, they wouldn't be poor." It is interesting that this is primarily an American/Canadian (rich country) doctrine because it won't preach anywhere else. Oft quoted in this book,

I Tim. 6:5 always comes to mind when I hear that: " . . . *men of corrupt mind, who have been robbed of the truth and who think that godliness is a means to financial gain."* As we have just read, almost all of the mentioning of giving after the ascension of Christ had to do with collections for the poor in Jerusalem.

Some ministers go so far as to take the idea from Malachi 3 about God blessing a person who gives the tithe and those who do not tithe being cursed, and they apply it to the very poor as well, so they will be excused from helping them. They ignore all the verses about tithing that discuss helping the poor with it. They ignore all the verses I have discussed that talk about a curse for those who do not help the poor. They deny the blessings stated in the Bible about helping those in need; and they ignore the fact mentioned above, that the main discussion of giving in the New Covenant is about giving to the poor. As an example of this, I want to tell a true story of one pastor I knew and how he treated a poor person in his church.

Over thirty years ago, I lived in a fairly small town and for a while went to the largest Assembly of God church there. There was a woman in that church who was shriveled and knotted up due to cerebral palsy. I will call her Molly (not her name). Molly could only move her left foot and toes a little and scooted herself around in her wheel chair with that left big toe. She could grab a pencil in her mouth and punch numbers on a telephone. She could talk plainly though and usually greeted people with a big smile. She loved Jesus and Elvis, in that order. Of course, someone had to bring her to church and back home.

Molly lived in a subsidized housing apartment because when she was in a nursing home she had been raped. She received a disability check and food stamps as her sole income. A social worker came to check on her regularly and arranged for a woman to come by and clean her apartment, but mainly to feed Molly and change her adult diaper twice a day. The church, to its credit, gave her $5 a week to help her buy vitamins that helped her energy level a lot. Molly had a little chihuahua dog that was her constant companion and the woman who came around would put down papers for the dog to do its business on.

The caretaker woman evidently got tired of cleaning up after the dog and said she would keep doing it, but needed $5 more a month to do so. Molly did not know what to do so she asked the pastor of the church if they could please help her out with that $5 extra a month. He got indignant and let her know she "did not even tithe." He basically told her she was lucky she got the $5 weekly she was getting. He was one of those who strongly believed that if you tithed, God would prosper you and if you did not, God would not and might bring a curse on you. He went as far as to apply that to this person who was helpless and at the mercy of others, the very type of person who God, in the Mosaic Covenant said the tithe was partly to provide for. By the way, the church as I recall, gave him a nice Lincoln, or maybe it was a Cadillac, car to drive around in. Molly was a friend of my wife and me and when we learned about what had been said and how the pastor reacted, we stopped going to that church and made sure she had the money she needed and a little extra. Molly did not live long after that. She has gone on to be with the Lord. I believe she gets around just fine now. If this pastor had studied all of what scripture taught about the tithe and other passages about helping the poor, as I bring out in this study, he would have understood that it was he who was not keeping the tithe laws, not her. The parable of the rich man and Lazarus comes to my mind regarding those two. That preacher may have been saved, but it is hard to see the love of God in him.

The New Testament example of sharing wealth among the church members (Acts 4:32-35) and the exhortation of one not having plenty while another has want (2 Cor. 8:13-15), are ignored by ministers and churches with the same excuse, that is, if they tithed and/or if they had enough faith, they would not be poor. Any prophet, patriarch, or preacher of Old Testament or New that went through times without worldly prosperity is attacked by these "followers of Balaam." In Ezekiel 14:14,20 Job is included with Noah and Daniel as one of the three most righteous men living up to that time, and yet men and women who are not worthy to wash his feet if he were here today, belittle him as not having had enough faith and attribute his problems to that. When crowns get passed out, we will be able to compare theirs with his, if they get one that is.

The many churches that pretend to want to go by the old covenant tithe laws (though as I have already stated, what is taught is not even accurate for the Mosaic Law) seem to be inconsistent in another way. The many part-time workers in the church, who equate to the old covenant Levites in many respects, are usually given nothing for their devoted and time-consuming efforts, even though their Old Testament equivalents were indeed helped out by the tithe. If a church really wants to be going by the old covenant tithe law, they should consider paying these modern-day Levites something. It was, after all (as you will remember from the verses you have read) the Levites who collected the tithe on the third year and brought one tenth of it (with a priest accompanying them) to the temple storerooms, keeping nine tenths of it as pay for their own work for God. Of course, there were many more Levites than priests and the Levites did not share in the other offerings which the priests received portions of, as part of their pay for the work at the altar. There was also a small fee imposed for maintenance of the house of God, which was separate from the tithe.

The fact is we are not under the law; however, we do take principles from each of the Old Testament covenants: the Adamic, the Abrahamic, and the Mosaic. We use these general principles of behavior along with the specific teachings of the inspired authors of the New Covenant to determine our doctrine and what we believe is right behavior. It is the principles found in the whole of scripture concerning the tithe that I am trying to bring to life here. Many denominations fault the Seventh Day Adventists for being legalistic about keeping the Mosaic Covenant's requirement to observe the Sabbath on Saturday. Non-Seventh Day Adventists point out that we are not under that covenant, so meeting on Sunday (the Lord's Day) is OK. What determines which Mosaic Covenant laws we have to keep and which ones we do not? In the case of tithing, I think it is obvious that it is because pastors think it benefits the church financially. If they legitimately believe that it is to be kept legalistically, then why don't they study and teach all that scripture says on the tithe instead of just the select few verses that fit their purposes? Unfortunately, I think the answer is too obvious to mention. Instead, by taking only a few verses by themselves, they wind up not teaching the Old Testament tithe law at all, but rather, something completely different, which more closely resembles the oppressive rules enforced by the political power of the Catholic Church and the Church of England in past centuries, which caused the confiscation of a tenth of all farmers' crops, than anything taught by scripture.

To be fair, I should say that many pastors went to Bible school or seminary and learned, not how to study and teach what the Bible teaches, but how to study and teach what their denomination teaches about the Bible. If they agreed with what I am writing whole-heartedly, most would not teach it because of fear of the wrath of their denomination (see the chapter on bullies in the pulpit). For those that just don't know any better, I hope this study helps.

Going back to the subject of giving to the poor, in "The Parable of the Sheep and the Goats," in Mt. 25:31-46, Jesus even divides the two groups of people for either eternal life or eternal punishment, based upon whether or not they had provided for those who had little or nothing. It is clear that Jesus is referring to salvation or damnation in this dividing of the sheep and goats. How much more important can giving to the poor be than determining salvation or damnation? It is not that one is saved by giving to the poor, but, if the love of God lives in us (whereby we know that we are saved), then we will be kind to the poor (especially poor Christians) and share with them what we have. First John 3:17 states: *"If anyone has material possessions and sees his brother in need but has no pity on him, how can the love of God be in Him?"* In 4:12 of that book John writes: *"No one has ever seen God; but if we love each other, God lives in us and his love is made complete in us."*

Returning to the idea of an individual seeking the Lord or spending time with the Lord, being important as related to tithing, look at a statement made in the Old Testament by the prophet Amos. Amos is prophesying doom to Israel when he mockingly says in 4:4-5;

> *"Go to Bethel and sin; go to Gilgal and sin yet more (these were places of sacrifice in Israel). Bring your sacrifices every morning, your tithes every three years. Burn leavened bread as a thank offering and brag about your freewill offerings -- boast about them you Israelites."*

Then he says in 5:4-6:

> *"This is what the Lord says to the house of Israel: "Seek me and live; do not seek Bethel, do not go to Gilgal, do not journey to Beersheba. For Gilgal will surely go into exile, and Bethel will be reduced to nothing. Seek the Lord and live, or he will sweep through the house of Joseph like a fire;"*

I think that this is saying that God wants us to seek Him, don't you? Some Christians today, believe that the pastor should do all the ministering, both to the world and to them. Many think that if they just give their ten percent and come to church, that is enough. The only time some "Christians" open their Bible is in Sunday school or church. The only time they pray is when they are in trouble or want something. This will not make them a part of the glorious church without spot or wrinkle. Christians need to be seeking God and extending his love to a hurting world.

SOME CONCLUSIONS AND COMMENTS

As I have stated already, more than once, a lot of preachers like to take part of II Cor. 9:7 and use it right before they take up the offering. They say "Remember, '… *God loves a cheerful giver.*'" Let's look again at the full verse for a moment:

> *Each of you should give what you have decided in your heart to give, not reluctantly or under compulsion, for God loves a cheerful giver.*

I wonder what the teaching of tithing in the common method (Malachi 3 only) is, if it is not compulsory giving? It seems like it is to me.

There were many offerings other than tithes that were given to God in the Old Testament. Some of these were required and some parts of these went to the priests and temple workers. Nehemiah chapter 10 mentions some of these and says some of them would be taken to the storerooms in the Temple. That said, each person must pray about how they feel they should divide up giving to the poor with giving to the church. Sometimes the churches give to the poor. Other times we are the only ones at the scene when a need arises that stirs the love of God in us and causes us to give money to a needy person or to share the good news of the Gospel with them. You may feel that you should still give it all to the church, but designate that some go to a specific person or needy group; giving to Christian children's "ranches" or orphanages certainly fulfills God's command to help the fatherless, as an example. We have a great Christian children's home in Alabama, called The Big Oak Ranch, which gladly accepts donations and deserves them. Some like to give to St. Jude Children's Hospital or to Shriner's Hospital for Children, to help with the care of sick children. James Robison, who I talked about earlier, has a great ministry called Life Outreach International, which provides clean water wells for villages around the world that need one and food for people around the world who need that, and freedom from sexual trafficking for some young people, mainly girls in Asia. Your money is well spent there. Samaritan's Purse is another great ministry by Franklin Graham and others, that most of you know about. Some people like to volunteer in and to give to prison outreach ministries. These are just a few options. You should pray about where God would like you to invest in the kingdom.

Honestly, I do not feel that needy people should be required to try to give to a church though, when they can't even feed themselves or pay their bills. This makes no sense to me because the church should, in love and obedience to God, be required to turn around and give it back with more added. The children of Israel did not have to give anything as a tithe while they were still in the desert. It was only after they had received their inheritance that giving was expected of them

(Dt. 12:9-11). The exception is when they contributed gold and other items for the construction of the tabernacle and its fixtures. God had made the Egyptians favorably disposed to them before they left, so they were given material goods by the Egyptians for this purpose.

As I have said, I know the argument that God will bless poor Christians' giving, but God knows that they can't afford to give and that His people should give it back so why do it to start with, especially since the passages on the tithe laws you have read in this study only discuss the poor being provided for, by the tithe, not in providing the tithe; and, as I have said, in my experience most churches do not even help their own poor in any significant manner. The church, whether collectively or as individuals should be trying to give to them. The church constantly overlooks this opportunity for ministry, or worse, turns its nose up at it. Laodicea is alive and well today (see Rev. 3:14-18).

It is the struggling and hurting person, often low on the financial ladder who is most ripe for the kingdom of God and in the most need of the fellowship of the saints and instruction in the Word of God. These people however, because of their financial struggles, are quickly made to feel that they do not fit in with the local church because even though they may be able to give something (and truly desire to do so), they can't see how they can give a tenth. If they are brave enough to continue going to church, they never really feel a whole part of it. I thought that Christians were supposed to be in the reconciliation business (II Cor. 5:18), not the alienation business. Instead we humiliate the poor and that for the idea that we will be a little better off financially as a church.

The truth is probably the opposite. If we helped the poor when help was needed and did not put such a burden on them but, rather, told them that when they were able to give and God led them to do so, they could give as God blessed them, then I think they would stay in the church more often, attend more regularly, get their lives more straightened out, and become spiritual blessings and even eventually, financial blessings to the church. We would certainly please God a whole lot more and we would avoid the curses God listed for failing to help the poor. It is these people God has called us to minister to. *"It is the sick that need a physician not the healthy."* A church without people to minister to is like a doctor with no patients: what is the purpose? The purpose is: let's have another "bless me club" with a prettier building than the "bless me club" down the street. Such churches should collectively read what I have already quoted before, about what Christ said to the church at Laodicea in Rev. 3:17-18:

> "You say, 'I am rich; I have acquired wealth and do not need a thing.' But you do not realize that you are wretched, pitiful, poor, blind and naked. I counsel you to buy from me gold refined in the fire, so you can become rich; and white clothes to wear, so you can cover your shameful nakedness; and salve to put on your eyes, so you can see."

Note again please, what Christ said to the church at Smyrna in Rev. 2:9:

> "I know your afflictions and your poverty---yet you are rich!"

As I quoted in the first part of this book, James, the Lord's half-brother wrote in James 2:1-9:

> "My brothers, as believers in our glorious Lord Jesus Christ, don't show favoritism. Suppose a man comes into your meeting wearing a gold ring and fine clothes, and a poor man in shabby clothes also comes in. If you show special attention to the man wearing fine clothes and say, 'Here's a good seat for you,' but say to the poor man, 'You stand there' or 'Sit on the floor by my feet,' have you not discriminated among yourselves and become judges with evil thoughts?
>
> Listen, my dear brothers; Has not God chosen those who are poor in the eyes of the world to be rich in faith and to inherit the kingdom he promised those who love him? But you have insulted the poor (underlining added). Is it not the rich who are exploiting you? Are they not the ones who

111

are dragging you into court? Are they not the ones who are slandering the noble name of him to whom you belong?

If you really keep the royal law found in Scripture, 'Love your neighbor as yourself,' you are doing right. But if you show favoritism, you sin and are convicted by the law as lawbreakers."

In closing, always remember that, when Paul wrote about giving to the poor, he said, "he who sows sparingly will reap sparingly" and God has not put any limit on offerings. Even though scripture does not say so, that probably applies to other offerings as well. I believe that everything we own, as believers, actually belongs to God and we will be judged based on what we have done with what we have. We should put our whole lives "as living sacrifices," on the altar to God (Rom. 12:1-2). We are talking here about becoming the Bride of Christ, beautifully dressed for her Husband and when he returns for us we will do well to be working with all of our abilities, heart, possessions, and time when he comes.

I am not saying that each of us is a pastor or evangelist, but we all have a ministry in the Kingdom and in his Army, we are all soldiers in a war. Every part of our lives should reflect that we are not our own, we are bought with a price. We should die daily to the fleshly desires that would cause us to selfishly invest our time and energies and wealth in useless things and instead invest them in the Kingdom where our riches are true riches. We should never limit our commitment to Christ to anything less than 100%; not 100% of our money of course, or else we would starve I suppose, not 100% of our time or we would neglect our families, jobs and so forth, but 100% of our lives.

By this, I mean that our lives should be lived in balance and purpose, gained by prayerfully seeking God's will, and by studying His Word and obeying it, to include helping the poor when we can, and stopping the practice of beating them up for tithes they can't afford, making them ashamed and angry and running them off from church (true shepherds don't scatter the flock, they care for and nurture the sheep). If we do all of these things the best we can, we will be on the path to "Becoming the Spotless Bride of Christ." Isn't that what you want to be? Pastors, on the other hand, who do not heed God's Word on this issue should be more than a little concerned about how God views their actions, as was quoted earlier in Ezekiel:

Ezekiel 34:2-4,10:

> *"Son of man, prophesy against the shepherds of Israel; prophesy and say to them: 'This is what the Sovereign Lord says: Woe to the shepherds of Israel who only take care of themselves! Should not shepherds take care of the flock? You eat the curds, clothe yourselves with the wool and slaughter the choice animals, but you do not take care of the flock. You have not strengthened the weak or healed the sick or bound up the injured. You have not brought back the strays or searched for the lost. (10) This is what the Sovereign Lord says: I am against the shepherds and will hold them accountable for my flock. I will remove them from tending the flock so that the shepherds can no longer feed themselves. I will rescue my flock from their mouths, and it will no longer be food for them.*

I believe that pastors who know what scripture says on this topic (they will if they have read this book and/or if they study the Bible) and they still refuse to teach tithing/giving, in a balanced way, are the biggest hypocrites in their churches. They are like the Pharisees of Jesus' time who cared more about the traditions of men than about the balanced Word of God. I would not want to be in their shoes on judgment day. Let him who has an ear hear.

GOVERNMENT AND CHURCH ENMESHED BOUNDARIES COMPLICATE GIVING

A major encroachment into church affairs by our Federal government took place around 1954 when the government revised tax laws to include the structuring of non-profit organizations. Frankly, I do not know much about what happened before that, but I am told Christians were allowed to deduct charitable contributions to churches from their taxable income before the 501(c) (3) revision took place. At any rate, churches were required (or thought they were) after this legislation became law, to organize as non-profits to be able to provide their contributors with documentation the IRS would accept for tax deduction claims on their annual filings. This gave churches a troublesome power in my way of thinking.

After this, churches that adopted the government non-profit status had the unscriptural task of keeping up with just how much each giver gave. Because by that time most people did their giving by writing a check, churches basically knew whether a person was tithing or giving something close to a tithe. Of course, givers could also take one of the giving envelopes from the pew and write in their name and the amount they were putting in the envelope if they wanted to give cash. Many pastors took note of who was or was not towing the line with what he/she was preaching about giving (usually the Malachi 3 by itself version of tithing). So not only do most pastors usually teach a false requirement about giving, they now can do more to try to push it.

This totally ignores the principles of not giving to be seen of men, but rather to give in secret so that your heavenly Father, who sees in secret, can reward you openly. This teaching from Matthew 6:1-2 also tells us that if we give to be seen by men, <u>we already have our full reward</u>. In some very foolish acting churches the pastors go so far as to have everyone who is giving above $100 (the amount may be higher) hold up their offering and come up front and put that in the offering, then those who are giving at least $75, and so forth. How stupid can people get? They act like they never saw a Bible, let alone read one. The pastors act like there is no fear of God in them. In churches that hold up the offerings by size like this and bring it down front so they can be seen of men and so they can shame those who don't give much or can't give at all, I don't understand how the pastors can be that corrupt and still preach a sermon. That is overtly and completely sinful and if you, the reader, go to a church like that (and I have been to a few briefly), I say leave it and, to paraphrase an old fashioned saying, don't let the screen door hit you on the backside on your way out. In other words, get out in a hurry. You can be sure that pastor is not worried about going by the Bible, or is just ignorant of it.

As part of acting as if they were helping church members out by keeping giving records, pastors and other leaders in the church assure members that this would help with the giver's taxes, providing them with a deduction. Well, that is only true, I found out, if those gifts and your other taxable itemized deductions added together, make up more than your standard deduction. For most church givers, even if they give a tithe, their deductions in total do not add up to more than the standard deduction for income tax purposes, so the records churches keep on them do not help them as a giver. However, there is a good possibility, I think, that letting people know how much they give, will keep them from getting heavenly rewards for the same. Sometimes the larger givers even try to influence the preachers because of their giving and threaten to leave the church and take their checkbook with them if the pastor does not do this or that. Ever see that?

As discussed already, in the book of James, chapter 2:1-9, it talks about if churches honor the rich person who comes into their service and dishonor the poor man who comes in, they have become judges with evil thoughts and are sinning.

I believe the way churches keep these records may sound good and logical, but in reality, it is a sick way of handling the offerings. It robs believers of a reward from God and probably is just one more thing that runs church goers away from church.

There is another problem with the 501(c)(3) status of churches. That is, they have to bring into the church, a non-Biblical form of organization. Instead of the five-fold ministry I discussed before, being the rule for church functioning and government, with the Biblical addition of deacons and deaconesses for practical operation, there is added to this now, a non-Biblical, Board of Directors with a President, Secretary, Treasurer, and other board members.

Senator, and later, Vice President, and then President, Lyndon B. Johnson, back in 1954, tacked on an amendment (called the Johnson Amendment) to the 501(c)(3) rules, that kept churches who were registered as non-profits from supporting political candidates. Churches have been limited to some degree from doing that ever since. Churches have however, produced "voter guides" that list where different candidates stand on important moral issues. Then church members could better decide for themselves who was the best candidate, in their minds, to do the job. Most people think LBJ was trying to keep churches back in his home state of Texas from supporting his opponent(s) because he was not very conservative. As you may know, Johnson later gave us the "great society" give away programs that have done so much damage to family structure, to general morals, and to the country as a whole. They continue to do this.

If any of you readers are planning to start a church of any kind in the future, I hope you will consider not forming a non-profit. Instead, consult a CPA or tax attorney in your area about what your other options are. I always try to give cash offerings, not inside any envelope, so the church leaders do not know what I am giving. It is none of their business what I give and I am not wanting to get my reward from them, but from my heavenly Father. If you are a leader in a church now, please consider anew how your church is organized and ask God to guide you about any changes you might make or encourage to be made.

LAST RECOMMENDATIONS

Now that you have read all of the book, except for probably the Appendix, I want to recommend some goals and plans for you to apply the principles I have talked about, to your life. The goalpost will continue to move in this process because you will continue to grow and achieve as a believer and student of the Word. Your ability to minister effectively will continue to grow and expand as you learn more and more. We never learn all there is to learn.

As you study to show yourself approved, you should continue to pray about goal adjustment. As you study, remember to use Content, Context, and Covenant, and the other interpretation principles, including all those in the Appendix. Learn to Recognize, Reject, and Replace false doctrine with doctrine that is supported by a balance of the entire Bible (rightly divided). In your giving, remember Galatians 2:10, "*All they asked was that we should continue to remember the poor, the very thing I had been eager to do all along.*"

A main goal is to develop a Bible reading plan so you can come to know what the Bible teaches on all doctrines in a balanced way for yourself. Remember that you are responsible for your own theology, not some preacher/pastor/evangelist etc. God can use these types of ministers if they are listening to Him, but too many are more in tune with their denominational ties and the leaven of the Pharisees (traditions of men taught as the commandments of God) than they are with the Holy Spirit. The Holy Spirit is the main Bible teacher and we can know precious little about the Bible without his help.

You will want to use a historically sequential reading plan (I listed a few of these in the book) at least for the first several times you read through the Bible. That helps it make more sense and helps you get a better idea of what actually happened in the Old Testament, especially. Books of Bible maps, timelines, and customs of the times are all helpful for you to build a more complete understanding of the Word. Be cautious though about commentaries because they have opinion in them and also may contain false doctrine. You probably want to use a modern language version of the Bible so you do not trip over the antiquated language of the KJV. If necessary, you could use The New KJV. It reads fairly smoothly and will not throw you off so much. I like the New American Standard Bible and the New International Version, but the latter has become gender neutral in recent editions, which is problematic to me, so I would go with the New American Standard Bible, the NASB. For those who want to be able to do Hebrew and Greek word studies, I suggest the Hebrew-Greek Key Word Study Bible, which comes in NASB and several other translations. It comes in hard back or leather and has key words numbered so you can turn to the built-in Old Testament and New Testament dictionaries in the back to look up the full definition of those words. The dictionary uses James Strong's Exhaustive Concordance Hebrew and Greek lexicon definitions and adds some to those. It also has a NASB concordance and many other study aids. It is produced by the American Mission to the Greeks, AMG, through AMG Publishers in Chattanooga, TN.

So, you need to read, read, read, and pray, pray, pray. Pray about what your calling is - what it is God is calling you to do and to become in your life of service to him. Open your heavenly bank account and begin to become rich in faith and in good deeds. You may want to consult with some godly person you know and respect and who can "disciple" and advise you as you move forward in your relationship with God. You can develop both short and long-range goals and remember to let yourself adjust these as you feel God guiding you to. Remember that God does not always provide the way we want, but he will provide the things we need to do his will. As the Apostle Paul said at the end of Ephesians, *"Grace be with all who love our Lord Jesus Christ with an undying love."*

APPENDIX

Bible Interpretation Principles (Hermeneutics): What Every Believer Needs to Know to Believe the Bible More and Understand it Better

I start this very important section of the book by establishing reasons why we study the Bible above all other books. After all, some people think the Bible only contains the Word of God and that not all of it is inspired by God. They believe it contains miracles that can't be explained by science so they are just mythological stories and not inspired. Many people, even in supposedly Christian colleges and seminaries, have been taught that the Bible is full of contradictions and even though it contains some very good things, not all of it can be trusted. If a person believes that not all the Bible is inspired by God, they will not worry about balancing the teachings of the Bible in an effective way. Once I cover proofs of inspiration, to some degree at least, I will follow with very important interpretation rules and guidelines.

Why do you put such faith in the Bible? What makes it more special than any other book? Other religions have books that they use to guide them. If I asked you today to defend why you want to base your life on a book that was admittedly written by men, could you do it? You might get kind of huffy and say, "Well, because it's the Word of God," and poke your nose defiantly in the air. I might then ask you, "Says who?" or say, "Give me some proof." Someone may offer, as many have in the past, the argument that the Bible contradicts itself and therefore could not possibly be from one mind, such as God's; it therefore is not something that they should base their life unconditionally on; it is merely a product of men, however well intentioned. If you have no answer for these arguments, then let me provide some. More important than winning an argument is the knowledge that we really can base our lives on this greatest of books because it is, in its original scripts, the inspired Word of God. The evidence I am providing for such a bold statement falls into five categories: the basic unity of the Bible, the fact that it proclaims unreservedly to be God's word, fulfilled prophecy within it, an unmistakable "ring of truth," and, the paradoxical balance explanation for seemingly conflicting passages.

Unity is the first of these categories. It is true that if various verses are taken away from their context and compared directly with other verses, we can find some astounding, seeming contradictions. In addition, some scripture, especially some of Paul's writings are just plain contradictive in their initial impact and are difficult to understand, sometimes even to those with a reasonable knowledge of the original text and the customs of the times. As is stated earlier in this book, Peter wrote in II Pet. 3:16:

> . . . *"His letters contain some things that are hard to*
> *understand, which ignorant and unstable people distort,*
> *as they do the other Scriptures, to their own destruction."*

Speaking of his contemporary (Paul), Peter admits there exists difficulty in interpretation but gives blame primarily to ignorance. I have found that people who have been indoctrinated into "High Calvinism" prior to gaining a good knowledge of scripture, have a hard time ever getting Paul figured out. I have found however, that where the understanding is most difficult to obtain, it is usually well worth the extra effort because the truths are more beautiful and profound than those which are more obvious. I will present some guidelines and suggestions for interpretation of difficult passages later; however, for those cases where scripture is simply not read in context, I offer the following ideas. The Bible is much like a large story book; it has a very beautiful subject; it is about God and His relationship with His creation, chiefly speaking, with mankind. This relationship deals with the immeasurable complexities of emotions, behavior, laws, agreements, and the remaining gamut of human experiences, each with its own set of variables and conditions. That is why it is so important that we read the Bible as though verse divisions were non-existent, using them merely for reference guides and not for anything else. Chapter and verse divisions were not even added to the Bible until long after its completion. When they were added, it was by a printer and it was done for the previously mentioned reasons, i.e., reference guides.

Please allow me to take a "rabbit trail" away from the unity theme for a moment to throw in some basic Bible interpretation guides. We should also ask ourselves as we read: 1. who is speaking, 2. what are they saying, and 3. how does this apply to me. We ask **who** is speaking because not everyone the Bible quotes is giving God's opinion, and because even if a person is speaking what God wants at the time, it may not apply to us directly in the New Covenant. An example of this is in the doing away of animal sacrifices by the sacrifice of the Lamb of God, Jesus. They were required in the past, but not now. In asking who is speaking, we should determine if it is an evil person or a godly person. If they are a Godly person or even a prophet, we should determine what covenant they were a part of and thus, is their teaching a direct requirement for today's reader or simply a general principle we can learn from and follow. Some Mosaic Covenant commands still apply to us today of course, such as the command not to commit murder. This ageless principle is written on the tablets of our hearts and minds by our Savior through the Holy Spirit.

Our consciences bear witness to the laws of the Holy Spirit, because they are the principles of love and of "doing unto others what we would have them do unto us." The command not to murder, not to commit adultery, and other such commands were based on the eternal principles of God's love and so apply through all covenants. This can't be said of most of the Mosaic commands which only served to point us toward the work of Christ and to be types and shadows of the real things that exist in our present covenant and in the one we will one day experience in God's presence. Prayer should always be made by the serious Bible student for insight and wisdom in the discerning of how anything written before the death, burial, and resurrection of Christ applies to us today.

In asking **what** they are saying, we also want to know scripture well enough to see how it relates to the rest of scripture. Even within one covenant, there are sometimes seeming contradictions and partial presentations of the whole truth on any particular subject. Only when you have read the Bible through a number of times, do balance and completeness begin to be built, not before. Knowing how one scripture passage balances another to bring out the whole picture is of course, impossible to do if you are new to the Bible. For new Bible students, that will have to come with time and diligent effort.

In asking **how** the things written apply to each of us today, as said before, we look at the covenant it was a part of and to what group it was targeted to. On the other hand, we should take as directly applying to our situations today, any teachings occurring after the new covenant began. The subject of understanding the Bible will be covered in more depth in the discussion of "paradox," later in this appendix. This "rabbit trail" on interpretation basics helps us remove potential detractors to the unity theme. That is why I chose to include it here rather than in the next part of this appendix, which is specifically on interpretation tools.

Moving back to the unity category of evidence, in regard to some people quoted in the Bible, not giving God's opinion, it is a fact that the Bible is full of such cases. For instance, God says of Job's "friends" that they did not speak what was right, and yet people quote from their orations as though this was God's teaching. Other people blasphemed God and are quoted in scripture. While it is true that they said those things, the things they said are not truth and the people are presented as liars. If you take a verse from the Bible that is quoting from one of their lies and say, "This is scripture so it is true," you will be very wrong.

When read as a true story interspersed with poetry, prophecy, and short insights into the relationship of God with certain individuals like Ruth and Job, we see an astounding unity, a singleness of purpose that can be best explained as the work of a single mind. Given the historical evidence that the Bible was written over such a long period of time, we must conclude that a supreme being was the possessor of this mind. The nature of this eternal being is part of the blessed message of scripture, as I state more fully later.

Self-proclamation is the next category of evidence for trusting scripture. Though perhaps not a proof, the fact that this book unreservedly states repeatedly that it is from God, i.e., "Thus saith the Lord," is noteworthy. Christ constantly quoted from the Old Testament and spoke of Old Testament events and patriarchs as historic facts and people, not subject to debate. One would then, have to doubt the deity and power of Jesus in order to doubt the inspiration of the "law and the prophets."

Fulfilled prophecy is another body of evidence. Perhaps the greatest proof of the inspiration of the scriptures, begins at the Adamic curse and goes through the last book of the Bible, Revelation. Since it would not be feasible to try to list all fulfilled prophecy, let me list a few concerning the messiah.

PROPHECY	FULFILLED
Gen. 3:15 (seed of a woman)	Ga. 4:4
Gen. 12:3 (seed of Abraham)	Mt. 1:1
Gen. 17:19 (seed of Isaac)	Lk. 3:34
Num. 24:17 (seed of Jacob)	Mt. 1:2
Gen. 49:10 (from the tribe of Judah)	Lk. 3:33
Is. 9:7 (heir to the throne of David)	Lk. 1:32,33
Mic. 5:2 (born in Bethlehem)	Lk. 2:4,5,7
Dan. 9:25 (time for His birth)	Lk. 2:1,2
Is. 7:14 (born of a virgin)	Lk. 1:26,27,30,31
Ps. 2:7 (declared the Son of God)	Mt. 3:17
Is. 61:1,2 (to heal the brokenhearted)	Lk. 4:18,19
Zech. 11:12 (sold for 30 silver pieces)	Mt. 26:15
Is. 53:5 (substitutionary sacrifice)	Rom. 5:6,8
Is. 53:12 (crucified with sinners)	Mk. 15:27,28
Zech. 12:10 (pierced hands and feet)	Jn. 20:27
Ps. 22:17,18 (soldiers gambled / coat)	Mt.27:35,36

Zech. 12:10 (his side pierced)	Jn. 19:34
Ps. 16:10, Ps. 49:15 (to be resurrected)	Mk. 16:6,7
Ps. 68:18 (His ascension to God's side)	Mk. 16:19, Ep. 4:8,
	I Cor. 15:4

A "ring of truth" is the next reason for faith in the Bible: The apostles wrote of Jesus, that no man spoke like Him. For He spoke as one having authority and not as one of the scribes. The written word has within it a power, a dynamic effect on the human heart, mind, and spirit.

Hebrews 4:12 says:

> *"For the word of God is living and active, sharper than any double-edged sword. It penetrates even to dividing soul and spirit."*

Read a chapter in a good novel, then read a chapter from the Bible in a "readable" translation, (the New American Standard Bible, the NASB, or the New International Version, the NIV, are good selections), you will begin to see that the authority and power which the apostles said existed in the speech of Christ, is apparent throughout the writings of God. Second Timothy 3:16-17 says:

> *All scripture is God-breathed and is useful for teaching, rebuking, correcting and training in righteousness, (17) so that the man of God may be thoroughly equipped for every good work."*

Second Peter 1:16-21 says:

> *"We did not follow cleverly invented stories when we told you about the power and coming of our Lord Jesus Christ, but we were eye-witnesses of his majesty. (17) For he received honor and glory from God the Father when the voice came to him from the Majestic Glory, saying, 'This is my Son, whom I love; with him I am well pleased.'*

(18) We ourselves heard this voice that came from heaven when we were with him on the sacred mountain. (19) And we have the word of the prophets made more certain, and you will do well to pay attention to it, as to a light shining in a dark place, until the day dawns and the morning star has risen in your hearts. (20) Above all, you must understand that no prophecy of Scripture came about by the prophets' own interpretation. (21) For prophecy never had its origin in the will of man, but men spoke from God as they were carried along by the Holy Spirit."

The next subject to discuss is <u>paradoxical truth</u>. Quoting from my old Merriam-Webster Dictionary, (Merriam-Webster Inc. 1986), definition of the word "paradox," we get some insight to the strength of the Bible, that to skeptic minds appears its weakness:

> "n. 1. Statement that may be true but seems to say two opposite things. `More haste, less speed' is a paradox."

Biblical doctrines are more often than not, made up of seemingly conflicting statements that are doing so in order that they might specifically, as clearly as possible, show the balance of a doctrine. To do this, many different lights must be shown upon the same moral rule (that is, the same principle must be shown being applied to many different conditions and situations) so that the full intention of God might be illuminated to the reader.

Note: I recommend the use of "The Victory Bible Reading Plan" for all those learning what the Bible is all about. This is because it lists the Old Testament in the order in which the events occurred by merging the historical and prophetic book divisions into a historically sequential listing. The Old Testament is especially not organized in a sequential way at all. Instead, it is organized into the general groupings of historical, poetical, and prophetical writings. Even some of the historical books overlap each other and some of the prophets were contemporaries of each other. It is a lot easier to make sense of the Bible narrative when the reader uses this historically sequential reading method. There are

Bibles that are organized in this manner so you could look for one of those to do your reading in. Another source for help in this is by Wycliffe Bible Translators. They produce a small book titled <u>Reading the Bible in Historical Sequence</u>. It is by Colin Candy and retails for $10 at the time of this writing. You can find it at wycliffenz.org. You can purchase "The Victory Bible Reading Plan" booklets I mentioned, from Amazon. com for about $10.

In addition to the who, what, and how questions, and the paradoxical truth principle, there are two more major principles we should apply to Bible interpretation if we really want to be workmen who are unashamed, and rightly dividing the Word of truth. <u>Understanding the nature of God</u> is probably the key component to understanding His Word. We do not serve the Greek or Roman gods who were supposedly petty, flawed and arbitrary in their imaginary natures. On the contrary, we serve a just and merciful and loving God. Once this concept is firmly established in our minds, we will not make some of the childish mistakes of interpretation some have made.

<u>The weight of scripture</u> is another principle to consider. Some people ignore vast quantities of scripture on a given Bible subject in order to find and twist to their liking, only a few scriptures. They do not arrive at the Biblical balance on a doctrine, but instead, they arrive at a position that conforms to what they want to believe and teach. We will examine both the nature of God and the weight of scripture principles as they relate to Bible interpretation. First, we will look at God's character, His nature, to see what kind of friend we have in heaven.

God never changes, people do (my paraphrased version of Mal. 3:6). The eternal principles of God's relationship with us never change. Covenants between God and man have changed but the principles stay the same because the nature of God is steadfast. Some Bible scholar "wannabees" who just take a very shallow view of things in the Bible, try to say that God is represented as harsh and cruel in the Old Testament, and as loving and merciful in the New Testament, and especially Christ's "Sermon on the Mount." They point to this as evidence that not all of the Bible is inspired. It should be said that such people, to begin with, do not approach the Bible with even an open mind or a "blank slate," let alone an attitude of faith. Instead, they approach it from the perspective of skepticism, looking for faults in order to justify unbelief. They do not look deeply enough to see the condition that brought on the harshness, and how long evil behavior continued before the judgment actually fell and how many warnings people got first. Old Testament judgments are physical warnings to us of God's judgment promised to New and Old Testament believers alike for evil living: Hell. Hell is mentioned much more in the New Testament than in the old. These Bible critics are ignorant, it seems, of the more subtle things in the Old Testament for when Christ taught his "Sermon on the Mount," he was quoting from, and expounding on, Old Testament passages: Is. 50:6, La. 3:30, Lv. 19:18, and Dt. 23:6, to mention a few. It is apparent then, that both mercy and judgment are found in both Testaments.

I would like for us to look closely at the "ways of God" (his nature), to help us understand the Bible. We are God's friends if we are trying to follow and serve him, and God reveals himself to his friends. In Jn. 15:15, Jesus says:

> *"I no longer call you servants, because a servant does not know his master's business. Instead, I have called you friends, for everything that I learned from my Father I have made known to you."*

An example of God revealing not only his plans, but also his nature is found in the next quote, when Moses appeals to him.

> Ex. 33:11-13; *"The Lord would speak to Moses face to face, as a man speaks with his friend. Then Moses would return to the camp, but his young aide Joshua son of Nun did not leave the tent. Moses said to the Lord, "You have been telling me, 'Lead these people,' but you have not let me know whom you will send with me. You have said, 'I know you by name, and you have found favor with me.' If you are pleased with me, teach me your ways so I may know you and continue to find favor with you. Remember that this nation is your people."*

Ex. 34:6-7a; *"And he passed in front of Moses, proclaiming, "The Lord, the Lord, the compassionate and gracious God, slow to anger, abounding in love and faithfulness, maintaining love to thousands, and forgiving wickedness, rebellion and sin."*

A New Testament verse that confirms this good nature of God is:

II Pet. 3:9; *"The Lord is not slow in keeping his promise, as some understand slowness. He is patient with you, not wanting anyone to perish, but everyone to come to repentance."*

The Psalms further discuss the goodness of God and give us more insight into this special revelation God gave to His friend Moses.

Ps. 99:4, 8; *"The King is mighty, he loves justice---you have established equity; in Jacob you have done what is just and right. O Lord our God, you answered them; you were to Israel a forgiving God, though you punished their misdeeds."*

Read also Ps.103:7; *"He made known his ways to Moses, his deeds to the people of Israel,"* (then in verse 8 the psalmist lists again the nature of God that God had revealed to Moses): *"The Lord is compassionate and gracious; slow to anger, abounding in love."*

Regarding the next to last verse (7), Moses knew why, as well as what, God wanted. The children of Israel only knew what (to do in the law). The people of Israel hardened their hearts, and therefore were unable to know God's ways, (Heb. 3:7-11).

I believe that the learning of God's ways gives us the light to understand the paradoxes in God's Word. Paul prayed for the knowledge of God so we could understand our hope, (and enter our rest) Eph. 1:17-18:

"I keep asking that the God of our Lord Jesus Christ, the glorious Father, may give you the Spirit of wisdom and revelation, so that you may know him better.

I pray also that the eyes of your heart may be enlightened in order that you may know the hope to which he has called you, the riches of his glorious inheritance in the saints,"

These truths are spiritually discerned. God wants to give his Spirit to everyone (Jn. 12:32), so they can understand his ways and walk in them by faith (Is. 2:3). The only thing in our way is our resistance, Heb. 3:15: *"As has just been said: 'Today, if you hear his voice, do not harden your hearts as you did in the rebellion.'"*

Open your hearts to God and pray for the knowledge of Him. As we read earlier, Peter says that Paul wrote difficult things to understand, but he goes on to say that growing in the knowledge of the Lord will keep you from falling into erroneous beliefs, II Pet. 3:16-18:

"He (Paul) writes the same way in all his letters, speaking in them of these matters. His letters contain some things that are `hard to understand, which ignorant and unstable people distort, as they do the other Scriptures, to their own destruction.

Therefore, dear friends, since you already know this, be on your guard so that you may not be carried away by the error of lawless men and fall from your secure position. But grow in the grace and knowledge of our Lord and Savior Jesus Christ. To him be glory both now and forever! Amen."

The knowledge of God's nature is at least one of the plumb lines God has given us to keep our doctrine straight and true. Consider the situation below. I am creating a changing condition between a father and son. The one constant is that the father loves his son. His love determines every response the father has toward his child in this changing situation.

First, the son unselfishly gives part of his allowance to a poor child who doesn't have enough money for lunch. The father found out about it and gave his son the same amount that evening, and even decided to slightly increase his son's allowance. The bad part of that is the son decides to start smoking, and with his additional money gets a man to buy cigarettes for him. The father finds a hidden cigarette butt and smells smoke on his child. He gives the boy a choice of losing his allowance for two months or getting a spanking and insists that the son quit smoking either way. The constant was love; the action changed from positive to negative based on the changing condition. God's discipline and mercy toward people works the same way.

A school teacher is taught to use both negative and positive consequences for behavior, in order to encourage good behavior and discourage the bad. This is, in both cases, for the good of the student. God deals with us in similar ways for our good.

I have mentioned praying as a way to know the attributes of God, but there are other things you may do also. Besides the prayers of Paul that we read earlier, I want to list 3 ways:

1. The first way to learn of God's attributes is to read of them in His Word. In addition to Ex. 34:6-7, and Ps. 103, read Rev. 19:11.

   I saw heaven standing open and there before me was a white horse, whose rider is called Faithful and True. With justice he judges and wages war.

It is clear that this is talking of Christ in whom all of the fullness of the Godhead dwelled. I get the picture from this verse that God is a pretty neat guy, don't you? Another good example comes from the book of Matthew 11:29:

   [29] Take my yoke upon you and learn from me, for I am gentle and humble in heart, and you will find rest for your souls.

2. The second action you can take to understand God's ways is to prove Him. I remember in grammar school, the teacher taught us how to

prove our answers in addition, by subtraction, and in multiplication, by division. Do God's actions toward His people and mankind in general, agree with what He claims of Himself? Let's look at my hypothetical situation for a minute. If that father had said "I love my son," but when the son did wrong, the father had laughed, the father would have made himself out to be a liar. He would actually have shown that he hated his son. Fortunately for us, our heavenly father's actions toward us are consistent with the good things he says of Himself.

After God had borne with much patience the iniquity of the Sodomites, he told Abraham that he was going to destroy Sodom. Abraham, in concern for the lives of the people, proclaimed to God, *"Far be it from thee to destroy the righteous with the wicked. Will not the judge of all the earth do right?"* Six questions followed (Gen. 18:16-32), making a total of seven, the number of completeness, and of God. Each time God answered one of the questions, he answered the first more emphatically, yes, Yes, YES. For 50, 45, 40, 30, 20 for even 10 righteous, he would not destroy the city; yes, Yes, YES, the judge of all the earth would do right!

3. The third way to learn the nature of God is to be as a child. The revelation of the Father in these days comes from the Son by the Spirit. Christ cautions us against trusting merely in academic effort, or even that combined with God given aptitude when it comes to getting to know the Father.

Matthew 11:25-27 (Amplified Vs.);

> *"At that time Jesus began to say, I thank You, Father, Lord of Heaven and earth, and acknowledge openly and joyfully to Your honor that you have hidden these things from the wise and clever and learned, and revealed them to babies -- to the childish, untaught and unskilled. Yes, Father, (I praise You that) such was Your gracious will and good pleasure. All things were entrusted and delivered to*

Me by My Father; and no one fully knows and accurately understands the Father except the Son and anyone to whom the Son deliberately wills to make Him known."

Take heart my friend. God has always hidden things from the proud and revealed them to the humble, that is, those who look to trust in him, acknowledging their own inabilities and limitations. Children on earth should trust and love their father. We, as children of God have such a wonderful heavenly Father, and he desires that we would have humble trust in and love toward him, that through his son, he might draw us to his bosom and reveal himself to us openly. Jesus and Moses have these testimonies of themselves; Mt. 11:29 (Amplified Vs.) *". . . for I am gentle (meek) and humble (lowly) in heart."* Ex. 12:3; *"Now the man Moses was very meek (gentle, kind and humble) or above all the men on the face of the earth."* Let our desire therefore be to be humble like them.

After the nature of God, I wanted to elaborate more on the <u>weight of scripture principle</u>. Even though this has been talked about some in other chapters, it is a major part of good Bible interpretation. Imagine reading a book. You read one or two pages where the mother in the story is said to have red hair by one of the characters. Everywhere else, however, on over 50 pages she is referred to as sandy blonde and the title is <u>My Blonde Mom</u>. Something is wrong isn't it? Closer examination may reveal that the times the red hair is mentioned, it was a very bright sunny day which could have revealed red highlights in her hair. Or perhaps the character remembers her from her youth when her hair had more reddish color in it. Because of the volume of print in favor of blonde hair, it would be foolish to say she had red hair and try to figure out why 50 places were not right instead of the two. Instead, the two "red" hair places help us see what shade of blonde she was.

There are certain doctrines in the Bible, such as the free will of man, and the great fairness of God that are main themes throughout the Bible. A few verses, though more than two, yet comparatively few, seem to contradict these doctrines. It concerns me that some people choose to accept and make doctrine out of a relatively few scriptures and try to explain away the bulk of scripture in so doing. It further concerns me that some of these contradictions, if not all, go against the nature of God. You should look at the "red haired" scripture, that is, the few verses that contradict what the much larger number of verses says, with common sense as to its place and with prayer and the knowledge of the nature of God, as to its interpretation. Of course, you must remember also the who, what, and how rules.

The principles found in this appendix are powerful tools to use while building your own balanced theology from the Word. We are all responsible to God for what we accept as correct Bible doctrine. If you simply accept everything I write or your preacher teaches and preaches, you are not doing right or being honorable. As I quoted earlier, the Bereans were considered more honorable than others because they searched the scriptures diligently to see if what Paul taught was correct (Acts 17:11). They did not even accept Paul at first because they were diligent and honorable. Is your preacher better than Paul? No! So, use these tools to help yourself get a balanced view of scripture, not taken from memorizing the "key" verses your denomination pushes, but taken from your own thorough and repeated study of the Word of God. Besides reading, you may want to listen to Bible CDs in the car or while getting dressed in the bathroom. Whatever works. If you are like me, you will have to make some adjustments to your theology as you become more knowledgeable. Also, don't forget to pray as you study. Ask God to give you understanding and wisdom as you read. The Holy Spirit is the best teacher and he desires to bring you into the knowledge and understanding of God and of his Word. Praise God! To quote Paul: *May the grace of the Lord Jesus Christ be with your spirit. Amen.*

Printed in the United States
By Bookmasters